Study Guide to Accompany

FOOD and BEVERAGE COST CONTROL

Fifth Edition

Lea R. Dopson   David K. Hayes

WILEY

JOHN WILEY & SONS, INC.

Published by John Wiley & Sons, Inc., Hoboken, New Jersey

Published simultaneously in Canada

For general information on our other products and services or for technical support, please contact our Customer Care Department within the United States at (800) 762-2974, outside the United States at (317) 572-3993 or fax (317) 572-4002.

Wiley also publishes its books in a variety of electronic formats. Some content that appears in print may not be available in electronic books. For more information about Wiley products, visit our web site at www.wiley.com.

Library of Congress Cataloging-in-Publication Data:

ISBN: 978-0-470-25139-3

Printed in the United States of America

10   9   8   7   6   5   4   3   2

Contents

To the Student

All foodservice managers, regardless of the type of operation they are involved in, must understand and manage the costs associated with operating their business. *Food and Beverage Cost Control, Fifth Edition* focuses on helping you with the study of cost management to understand its logic and its systems.

The authors find the challenge of cost management to be creative, exciting, and fun! To be successful, talented foodservice managers must know where they want to take their operations and then apply their training and expertise to get there. In that regard, a professional hospitality manager is much like an airline pilot. Both utilize highly specialized skills and equipment. Both depend on other team members to reach their goals. Both must master a highly specialized area of study.

This *Study Guide* is intended to provide you with the first step in what will be a lifelong and financially rewarding study of how to reach new heights in your management of food and beverage costs. The *Study Guide* is organized according to the 12 chapters in the text. Each chapter provides the following student's aids:

- Learning Outcomes
- Study Notes
- Key Terms & Concepts Review
- Discussion Questions
- Quiz Yourself

The *Study Notes* are intended to help you better understand the content. The answers to *Key Terms & Concepts Review*, *Discussion Questions*, and *Quiz Yourself* are provided at the end of each chapter. All the information in this *Study Guide* can be used for reviewing the material and for testing your grasp of cost control concepts and techniques.

Special thanks go to Raktida Siri who assisted us with the *Study Guide*. We hope that this exposure to the study of cost management creates in you the same enjoyment that we have experienced in our careers. If so, the skills and tools you learn will ensure that your hospitality career will really take off, allowing you to go wherever you want to go and as high as you want to go!

Good luck!

Lea R. Dopson
David K. Hayes

Chapter 1

Managing Revenue and Expense

Learning Outcomes

At the conclusion of this chapter, you will be able to:

- Apply the basic formula used to determine profit.

- Express both expenses and profit as a percentage of revenue.

- Compare actual operating results with budgeted operating results.

Study Notes

1. Professional Foodservice Manager

- A professional foodservice manager is unique because all the functions of product sales, from item conceptualization to product delivery are in the hands of the same individual.

- Because foodservice operators are in the service sector of business, many aspects of management are more difficult for them than for their manufacturing or retailing management counterparts.

- A foodservice manager is one of the few types of managers who actually has contact with the ultimate consumer. The foodservice operator must serve as a food factory supervisor, and a cost control manager.

- Excellence in operation is measured in terms of producing and delivering quality products in a way that assures an appropriate operating profit for the owners.

2. Profit: The Reward for Service

- If management focuses on controlling costs more than on servicing guests, problems will certainly surface.

- Management's primary responsibility is to deliver a quality product or service to the guest, at a price mutually agreeable to both parties. You do not want to get yourself in the mind-set of reducing costs to the point where it is thought that "low" costs are good, and "high" costs are bad.

- When management attempts to reduce costs, with no regard for the impact on the balance between managing costs and guest satisfaction, the business will surely suffer. Efforts to reduce costs that result in unsafe conditions for guests or employees are never wise.

- The question is whether costs are too high or too low, given management's view of the value it hopes to deliver to the guest and the goals of the foodservice operation's owners.

- The difference between what you have paid for the goods you sell and the price at which you sell them does not represent your actual profit.

- **Revenue** is the amount of dollars you take in.

- **Expenses** are the costs of the items required to operate the business.

- **Profit** is the amount of dollars that remain after all expenses have been paid.

$$\text{Revenue} - \text{Expenses} = \text{Profit}$$

- For the purposes of this book, the authors will use the following terms interchangeably: revenue and sales; expenses and costs.

- All foodservice operations, including non-profit institutions, need revenue in excess of expenses if they are to thrive.

- Profit is the result of solid planning, sound management, and careful decision-making.

$$\text{Revenue} - \text{Desired Profit} = \text{Ideal Expense}$$

- **Ideal Expense** is defined as management's view of the correct or appropriate amount of expense necessary to generate a given quantity of revenue.

- **Desired profit** is defined as the profit that the owner wants to achieve on that predicted quantity of revenue. Profit is the reward for providing service.

- Revenue varies with both the number of guests frequenting your business and the amount of money spent by each guest.

- You can increase revenue by increasing the number of guests you serve, by increasing the amount each guest spends, or by a combination of both approaches.

- Environmental sustainability is a term used to describe a variety of earth-friendly practices and policies designed to meet the needs of the present population without compromising the ability of future generations to meet their own needs.

- The positive benefits that accrue when businesses incorporate green activities are significant and they are increasing.

- There are four major foodservice expense categories that you must learn to control.
    a. **Food costs** are the costs associated with actually producing the menu items. In most cases, food costs will make up the largest or second largest expense category you must learn to manage.
    b. **Beverage costs** are those related to the sale of alcoholic beverages. Costs of a non-alcoholic nature are considered an expense in the Food Costs category. Alcoholic beverages accounted for in the Beverage Costs category include beer, wine, and liquor. It may also include the costs of ingredients necessary to produce these drinks, such as cherries, lemons, olives, limes, mixers like carbonated beverages and juices, and other items commonly used in the production and service of alcoholic beverages.
    c. **Labor costs** include the cost of all employees necessary to run the business, including taxes. In most operations, labor costs are second only to food costs in total dollars spent. Some operators find it helpful to include the cost of management in this category. Others prefer to place the cost of managers in the Other Expense category.
    d. **Other expenses** include all expenses that are neither food, beverage nor labor.

3. Getting Started

- Good managers learn to understand, control, and manage their expenses. Numbers can be difficult to interpret due to inflation. Therefore, the industry uses percentage calculations.

- Percentages are the most common standard used for evaluating costs in the foodservice industry. As a manager in the foodservice industry you will be evaluated primarily on your ability to compute, analyze, and control these percent figures.

- **Percent** (%) means "out of each hundred."

- There are three (3) ways to write a percent:

Common Form
In its common form, the "%" sign is used to express the percentage, as in 10%.

Fraction Form
In fraction form, the percent is expressed as the part, or a portion of 100, as in 10/100.

Decimal Form
The decimal form uses the decimal point (.) to express the percent relationship, as in 0.10.

- To determine what percent one number is of another number, divide the number that is the part by the number that is the whole.

$$\frac{\text{Part}}{\text{Whole}} = \text{Percent}$$

- If we want to know what percentage of our revenue went to pay for our expenses, we would compute it as follows:

$$\frac{\text{Expense}}{\text{Revenue}} = \text{Expense \%}$$

- As long as expense is smaller than revenue, some profit will be generated. You can computer profit % using the following formula:

$$\frac{\text{Profit}}{\text{Revenue}} = \text{Profit \%}$$

- Modified profit formula:

Revenue – (Food and Beverage Cost + Labor Cost + Other Expenses) = Profit

- Put in another format, the equation looks as follows:

> **Revenue (100%)**
> - **Food and Beverage Cost %**
> - **Labor Cost %**
> - **Other Expense %**
> = **Profit %**

4. Understanding the Income (Profit and Loss) Statement

- An accounting tool that details revenue, expenses and profit, for a given period of time, is called the **income statement**, commonly referred to as a **profit and loss statement (P&L).** It lists revenue, food and beverage cost, labor cost, other expense, and profit.

- The P&L is important because it indicates the efficiency and profitability of an operation.

- The primary purpose of preparing a P&L is to identify revenue, expenses, and profits for a specific time period.

- Common percentages used in a P&L statement:

  1. $$\frac{\text{Food and Beverage Cost}}{\text{Revenue}} = \textbf{Food and Beverage Cost \%}$$

  2. $$\frac{\text{Labor Cost}}{\text{Revenue}} = \textbf{Labor Cost \%}$$

  3. $$\frac{\text{Other Expense}}{\text{Revenue}} = \textbf{Other Expense \%}$$

  4. $$\frac{\text{Total Expense}}{\text{Revenue}} = \textbf{Total Expense \%}$$

  5. $$\frac{\text{Profit}}{\text{Revenue}} = \textbf{Profit \%}$$

- The Uniform System of Accounts is used to report financial results in most foodservice units. This system was created to ensure uniform reporting of financial results.

5. Understanding the Budget

- A **budget** is simply an estimate of projected revenue, expense, and profit.

- The budget is known as the **plan**, referring to the fact that the budget details the operation's estimated, or planned for, revenue and expense for a given period of time.

- All effective managers, whether in the commercial (for profit) or nonprofit sector, use budgets.

- **Performance to budget** is the percentage of the budget actually used.

- The **28-day-period approach** to budgeting divides a year into 13 equal periods of 28 days each. This helps the manager compare performance from one period to the next without having to compensate for "extra" days in any one period.

- Percentages are used to compare actual expense with the budgeted amount, using the formula

$$\frac{\text{Actual}}{\text{Budget}} = \% \text{ of Budget}$$

- If our budget was accurate, and we are within reasonable limits of our budget, we are said to be "in-line" or "in compliance" with our budget. Use the concept of "significant" variation to determine whether a cost control problem exists.

- A significant variation is any variation in expected costs that management feels is an area of concern.

- If significant variations with planned results occur, management must:

  1. Identify the problem
  2. Determine the cause
  3. Take corrective action

6. Technology Tools

- Most hospitality managers would agree that an accurate and timely income statement (P&L statement) is an invaluable aid to their management efforts. There are a variety of software programs on the market that can be used to develop this statement for you.

- Variations include programs that compare your actual results to budgeted figures or forecasts, to prior-month performance, or to prior-year performance. In addition, P&Ls can be produced for any time period, including months, quarters, or years. Most income statement programs will have a budgeting feature and the ability to maintain historical sales and cost records.

- As you examine (in this chapter and others) the cost control technology tools available to you, keep in mind that not all information should be accessible to all parties, and that security of your cost and customer information can be just as critical as accuracy.

- Don't forget that to effectively manage your overall operation you will need to communicate with employees, guests, and vendors. Thus, the software you will need includes office products for word processing, spreadsheet building, faxes, and e-mail.

Key Terms & Concepts Review

Match the key terms with their correct definitions.

1. Revenue _____   a. A period of time, that is, hour, day, week, or month, in which an operator wishes to analyze revenue and expenses.

2. Expense _____   b. A detailed listing of revenue and expenses for a given accounting period. Also referred to as a profit and loss (P&L) statement.

3. Profit _____   c. The dollar costs associated with actually producing the menu item(s) a guest selects.

4. Business dining _____   d. The term used to indicate the dollars taken in by the business in a defined period of time. (Often referred to as sales.)

5. Ideal expense _____   e. Food is provided as a service to the company's employees either as a no-cost (to the employee) benefit or at a greatly reduced price.

6. Desired profit _____   f. The expenses of an operation that are neither food, beverage, nor labor.

7. Environmental sustainability _____   g. Accounting method that divides a year into 13 equal periods of 28 days each.

8. Food costs _____   h. The price paid to obtain the items required to operate the business. (Often referred to as costs.)

9. Beverage costs _____   i. The number "out of each hundred." Thus, 10 percent means 10 out of each 100. This is computed by dividing the part by the whole.

10. Labor costs _____   j. The profit that an owner seeks to achieve on a predicted quantity of revenue.

11. Other expenses _____   k. The percent of the budget actually spent on expenses.

12. Percent _____   l. The dollars that remain after all expenses have been paid. (Often referred to as net income.)

13. Income statement _____   m. A forecast or estimate of projected revenue, expense, and profit for a defined accounting period.

14.	Profit and loss statement (P&L)	_____	n.	Management's view of the correct or appropriate amount of expense necessary to generate a given quantity of sales.
15.	Uniform System of Accounts	_____	o.	The costs related to the sale of alcoholic beverages.
16.	Budget/Plan	_____	p.	A detailed listing of revenue and expenses for a given accounting period. Also referred to as an income statement.
17.	Accounting period	_____	q.	All expenses (costs), including payroll, required to maintain a workforce in a foodservice operation.
18.	Performance to budget	_____	r.	Standardized sets of procedures used for categorizing revenue and expense in a defined industry, for example, *Uniform System of Accounts for Restaurants (USAR)*.
19.	28-day-period approach	_____	s.	A variety of earth-friendly practices and policies designed to meet the needs of the present population without compromising the ability of future generations to meet their own needs.

Discussion Questions

1. List and determine (yes/no) the different tasks in which foodservice, manufacturing, and retailing managers vary in responsibility.

Task	Foodservice Manager	Manufacturing Manager	Retail Manager

2. List and explain the three different forms of writing a percent.

100% - a 1.0 - 100/100

_____

_____

_____

_____

8

3. List and explain what the four major foodservice expense categories are.

F/B, Labor, Other, total

4. List the three things a foodservice manager should do when there is a significant variation in the operation.

1.) Identify the problem 2.) Determine the cause 3.) take Corrective action

5. List two positive benefits that accrue when businesses incorporate green activities.

Sustainablity, tax brakes

Quiz Yourself

Choose the letter of the best answer to the questions listed below.

Questions 1, 2, 3, and 4 are based on the following information:
A simplified annual P & L statement for The Limpopo River House is shown below:

Description	Dollars	Percentages
Revenues	$1,200,000	
Food & Beverage Costs	$375,000	
Labor Costs	425,000	
Other Costs	100,000	
Total Expense		
Profit		

1. What was the profit expressed as a percentage for The Limpopo River House?
   a. 16.25%
   b. 25.00%
   c. 37.50%
   d. 63.50%

2. If the desired profit for this level of annual revenues was 18.00%, what was the ideal expense?
   a. $100,250
   b. $216,000
   c. $984,000
   d. $568,150

3. If the budget for food and beverage costs was $320,000, what was the budgeted food and beverage cost percentage and what was the percent of budget?
   a. The budgeted food and beverage cost percentage was 26.67% and the percent of budget was 117.19%.
   b. The budgeted food and beverage cost percentage was 37.50 % and the percent of budget was 102.21%.
   c. The budgeted food and beverage cost percentage was 50% and the percent of budget was 8.34%.
   d. The budgeted food and beverage cost percentage was 60% and the percent of budget was 3.25%.

4. If the budget for labor costs was $465,000, what was the performance to budget?
   a. 109.4%
   b. 91.4%
   c. 130.0%
   d. 39.6%

5. Matt Dain is a foodservice manager. Last month his food expense equaled $60,000, his labor expense equaled $50,000, and his other expenses equaled $19,000. His revenue equaled $160,000. What is his total expense percentage?
   a. 78.2%
   b. 120.0%
   c. 80.6%
   d. 35.8%

6. What is the formula to calculate profit percentage?
   a. Revenues – Expenses
   b. Expenses/ Profit
   c. Revenue/ Sales
   d. Profit/ Revenues

7. What formula would be used to calculate food and beverage cost percentage?
   a. Food and beverage expense/ revenue
   b. Food and beverage expense/ total expenses
   c. Total revenue – food and beverage expense
   d. Total expenses – food and beverage expense

8. What formula would be used to calculate percent of budget?
   a. Revenue/ Budget
   b. Revenue/ Actual
   c. Actual/ Budget
   d. Budget/ Actual

9. Which of the following is the labor cost percent formula?
   a. Labor expense/ revenues
   b. Number of employees/ total revenues
   c. Revenues/ labor expenses
   d. None of the Above

10. What is the formula to calculate other expense percent?
    a. Total revenue – other expense
    b. Other expense/ total expenses
    c. Other expense/ revenue
    d. Total expenses – other expenses

11. Jackie Wong is a foodservice manager. Last month his food expense equaled $65,000, his labor expense equaled $53,000, and his other expenses equaled $17,000. His revenue equaled $200,000. What is his profit percentage?
    a. 32.50%
    b. 0.32%
    c. 3.07%
    d. 68.5%

12. Ginger Lee is a foodservice manager. Last month her food expense equaled $70,000, her labor expense equaled $50,000, and her other expenses equaled $15,000. Her revenue equaled $200,000. What is her other expenses percentage?
    a. 0.07%
    b. 7.50%
    c. 13.00%
    d. 93.00%

Chapter Answers to Key Terms & Concepts Review, Discussion Questions, and Quiz Yourself

Key Terms & Concepts Review

1. d	5. n	9. o	13. b	17. a
2. h	6. j	10. q	14. p	18. k
3. l	7. s	11. f	15. r	19. g
4. e	8. c	12. i	16. m	

Discussion Questions

1. List and determine (yes/no) the different tasks in which foodservice, manufacturing, and retailing managers vary in responsibility.

Task	Foodservice Manager	Manufacturing Manager	Retail Manager
1. Secure raw materials	Yes	Yes	No
2. Manufacture product	Yes	Yes	No
3. Distribute to end-user	Yes	No	Yes
4. Market to end-user	Yes	No	Yes
5. Reconcile problems with end-user	Yes	No	Yes

2. List and explain the three different forms of writing a percent.
   - Common Form - In its common form, the "%" sign is used to express the percentage, as in 10%.
   - Fraction Form - In fraction form, the percent is expressed as the part, or a portion of 100, as in 10/100.
   - Decimal Form - The decimal form uses the decimal point (.) to express the percent relationship, as in 0.10.

3. List and explain what the four major foodservice expense categories are.
   - **Food costs** include the expense of meats, dairy, fruits, vegetables, and other categories of food items produced by the foodservice operation.
   - **Beverage costs** include alcoholic beverages of beer, wine, and liquor.
   - **Labor costs** include the cost of all employees necessary to run the business, including taxes.
   - **Other expenses** include all expenses that are neither food, nor beverage, nor labor. Examples include franchise fees, utilities, rent, linen, china, glassware, kitchen knives, and pots and pans.

4. List the three things a foodservice manager should do when there is a significant variation in the operation.
    - Identify the problem.
    - Determine the cause.
    - Take corrective action.

5. List two positive benefits that accrue when businesses incorporate green activities.
    - Managers of Green operations help protect the environment.
    - Customers are committed to preserving the environment and seek to support businesses that are committed to this as well.

Quiz Yourself

1. b	7. a
2. c	8. c
3. a	9. a
4. b	10. c
5. c	11. a
6. d	12. b

Chapter 2

Determining Sales Forecasts

Learning Outcomes

At the conclusion of this chapter, you will be able to:

- Develop a procedure to record current sales.

- Compute percentage increases or decreases in sales over time.

- Develop a procedure to predict future sales.

Study Notes

1. Importance of Forecasting Sales

- The first question operating managers must ask themselves is very simple: "How many guests will I serve today?" - "This week?" - "This year?" The answer to questions such as these are critical, since these guests will provide the revenue from which the operator will pay basic operating expenses and create a profit.

- In an ongoing operation, it is often true that future sales estimates, or projected sales, will be heavily based upon your sales history since what has happened in the past in your operation is usually the best predictor of what will happen in the future.

- A **sales forecast** predicts the number of guests you will serve and the revenues they will generate in a given future time period.

- You can determine your actual sales for a current time period by using a computerized system called a **point of sales (POS) system** that has been designed to provide specific sales information.

- Remember that a distinction is made in the hospitality industry between sales (revenue), and **sales volume**, which is the number of units sold.

- Sales may be a blend of cash and non-cash.

- With accurate sales records, a sales history can be developed for each foodservice outlet you operate and better decisions will be reached with regard to planning for each unit's operation.

2. Sales History

- **Sales history** is the systematic recording of all sales achieved during a predetermined time period. Sales histories can be created to record revenue, guests served, or both.

- **Sales to date** is the cumulative total of sales reported in the unit.

- An **average or mean** is defined as the value arrived at by adding the quantities in a series and dividing the sum of the quantities by the number of items in the series.

- The two major types of averages you are likely to encounter as a foodservice manager are as follows:

  o **Fixed average** is an average in which you determine a specific time period, for example, the first fourteen days of a given month, and then you compute the mean or average amount of sales or guest activity for that period.

  o **Rolling average** is the average amount of sales or volume over a changing time period. Essentially, where a fixed average is computed using a specific or constant set of data, the rolling average is computed using data that will change.

- The use of the rolling average, while more complex and time consuming than that of a fixed average, can be extremely useful in recording data to help you make effective predictions about the sales levels you can expect in the future.

- **Guest count** is the term used in the hospitality industry to indicate the number of people you have served, and is recorded on a regular basis.

- When managers record both revenue *and* guest counts, information needed to compute **average sales per guest**, a term also known as **check average**, is provided.

$$\frac{\text{Total Sales}}{\text{Number of Guests Served}} = \text{Average Sales per Guest}$$

- Most POS systems report the amount of revenue you have generated in a selected time period, the number of guests you have served, and the average sales per guest. Of course, the same data could be compiled manually.

- A **weighted average** is an average that weights the number of guests with how much they spend in a given time period.

- The weighted average sales per guest for 2 days is as follows:

$$\frac{\text{Day 1 Sales} + \text{Day 2 Sales}}{\text{Day 1 Guests} + \text{Day 2 Guests}} = \frac{\text{Two Day}}{\text{Average Sales per Guest}}$$

3. Maintaining Sales Histories

- Sales history may consist of revenue; number of guests served, and average sales per guest. You may want to use even more detailed information, such as the number of a particular menu item served, the number of guests served in a specific meal or time period, or the method of meal delivery (for example, drive-through vs. counter sales).

- In most cases, your sales histories should be kept for a period of at least two years.

- **Sales variances** are changes from previously experienced sales levels.
  (See figure 2.9)

- The variance is determined by subtracting sales last year from sales this year.

$$\text{Sales This Year} - \text{Sales Last Year} = \text{Variance}$$

- **Percentage variance** indicates the percentage change in sales from one time period to the next.

$$\frac{\text{Sales This Year} - \text{Sales Last Year}}{\text{Sales Last Year}} = \text{Percentage Variance}$$

or

$$\frac{\text{Variance}}{\text{Sales Last Year}} = \text{Percentage Variance}$$

or

$$\frac{\text{Sales This Year}}{\text{Sales Last Year}} - 1 = \text{Percentage Variance}$$

4. Predicting Future Sales

- Depending on the type of facility you manage, you may be interested in predicting, or forecasting, future revenues, guest counts, or average sales per guest levels.

- Revenue forecast is calculated using the following formula:

> **Sales Last Year + (Sales Last Year x % Increase Estimate) = Revenue Forecast**

or

> **Sales Last Year x (1 + % Increase Estimate) = Revenue Forecast**

- Use the revenue increases you have experienced in the past to predict increases you may experience in the future.

- Using the same techniques employed in estimating increases in sales, the non-cash operator or any manager interested in guest counts can estimate increases or decreases in the number of guests served.

- The guest count forecast is determined by multiplying guest count last year by the % increase estimate, and then adding the guest count last year.

> **Guest Count Last Year + (Guest Count Last Year x % Increase Estimate) = Guest Count Forecast**

or

> **Guest Count Last Year x (1.00 + % Increase Estimate) = Guest Count Forecast**

- Average sales per guest (check average) is simply the average amount of money each guest spends during a visit.

- Using data taken from the sales history, the following formula is employed:

> **Last Year's Average Sales per Guest**
> **+ Estimated Increase in Sales per Guest**
> **= Sales per Guest Forecast**

- An average sales per guest forecast is obtained by dividing the revenue forecast by the guest count forecast.

$$\frac{\text{Revenue Forecast}}{\text{Guest Count Forecast}} = \text{Average Sales per Guest Forecast}$$

- It is important to note that sales histories, regardless of how well they have been developed and maintained, are not sufficient, used alone, to accurately predict future sales.

- Your knowledge of potential price changes, new competitors, facility renovations, and improved selling programs are just a few of the many factors that you must consider when predicting future sales.

- Guest counts can be increased by undertaking green initiatives. It is important to market the products and services directly to the rapidly growing market segment of educated, savvy customers who care about the food they eat and their impact on the world around them.

- Implementing sustainable practices that focus on conservation as well as utilizing organic, seasonal, and locally grown products can help build customer and employee loyalty, as well as boost profits.

5. Technology Tools

- The importance of accurate sales histories for use in forecasting future sales is unquestionable. Your POS system can be invaluable in this effort. Many systems today can be utilized to do the following:

  1. Track sales by guest count
  2. Track sales by date
  3. Monitor cash vs. credit sales
  4. Maintain products sold histories
  5. Maintain check average data
  6. Compare actual sales to prior-period sales
  7. Maintain rolling sales averages
  8. Forecast future sales in increments
  9. Maintain actual sales to forecasted sales variance reports
  10. Maintain reservations systems

- For those operations that rely on reservations to control bookings, software of this type is available to instantly identify repeat guests, giving the operator a display screen that can include such information as frequency of visit, purchase preferences, and total dollars spent in the operation.

- Reservations software makes it possible for operators to reward repeat guests by developing their own "frequent dining" programs, similar to a hotel or airlines' frequent-traveler programs.

- Customer complaints can be tracked and, if desired, coupons to compensate guests for difficulties can be printed and distributed.

- Reservations-related programs such as these can store information on reservation demand, predict optimal reservation patterns, identify frequent no-show guests, and even allow guests to make their own reservations via on-line Internet connections.

Key Terms & Concepts Review

Match the key terms with their correct definitions.

1. Sales forecast/projected sales _____   a. The process of reporting a time period for which records are being maintained. This may be of the same duration as an accounting period.

2. Point of sales (POS) system _____   b. An average that combines data on the number of guests served and how much each has spent during a given financial accounting period.

3. Sales volume _____   c. A prediction of the number of guests to be served and the revenues they will generate in a defined, future time period.

4. Sales history _____   d. The average amount of sales or volume over a changing time period, for example, the last ten days or the last three weeks.

5. Sales to date _____   e. The number of units sold.

6. Reporting period _____   f. The change in sales, expressed as a percentage, that results from comparing two operating periods.

7. Average (mean) _____   g. The value arrived at by adding the quantities in a series and dividing the sum of the quantities by the number of items in the series.

8. Fixed average _____   h. A record of sales achieved by an operator in a given sales outlet during a specifically identified time period.

9. Rolling average _____   i. The mean amount of money spent per customer during a given financial accounting period. (Often referred to as check average.)

10. Guest count _____   j. An increase or decrease from previously experienced or predicted sales levels.

21

11. Average sales per guest _____ k. A system for controlling
    (check average)   hospitality operations' cash and
                                         product usage by using a
                                         computer processor and,
                                         depending on the size of the
                                         operation, additional computer
                                         hardware, communications
                                         devices and/or software.

12. Weighted average _____   l. The cumulative sales figures
                                  reported during a given financial
                                  accounting period.

13. Sales variance _____   m. The number of individuals
                                served in a defined time period.

14. Percentage variance _____   n. The average amount of sales or
                                     volume over a specific series or
                                     time period; for example, first
                                     month of the year or second
                                     week of the second month.

Discussion Questions

1. List and explain what the two major types of averages a foodservice manager may
encounter and what their formulas are to solve them.

_____
_____
_____
_____

2. List three different types of information that may be used for maintaining sales
histories.

_____
_____
_____
_____

3. Determine what three parts may be involved in predicting future sales.

_____
_____
_____
_____

4. Determine five advantages that are involved with sales forecasts.

_____
_____
_____
_____

5. List two examples of green practices that can help build customer and employee loyalty, as well as boost profits of foodservice operations.

_____
_____
_____
_____

Quiz Yourself

Choose the letter of the best answer to the questions listed below.

1. Calculate average sales per guest given the following information: total sales $156,200; number of guests served 3,500; total expenses $25,632.
    a. $ 44.63
    b. $123.25
    c. $ 25.98
    d. $ 65.23

2. Using the following information compute percentage variance: variance $3,200; sales last year $68,263.
    a. 2.54%
    b. 24.21%
    c. 4.69%
    d. 15.36%

3. Use the following information to calculate average sales per guest forecast: revenue forecast $102,500; guest count forecast 25,000.
    a. $5.50
    b. $4.10
    c. $8.25
    d. $6.99

4. Using the following information, calculate the two-day average sales per guest: Monday sales $5,265; Tuesday sales $3,987; Monday guests 500; Tuesday guests 400.
    a. $25.36
    b. $15.98
    c. $ 8.26
    d. $10.28

5. Calculate sales variance using the following information: sales last year $359,265; sales this year $245,968.
    a. $ -113,297
    b. $ 113,297
    c. $ 2,987
    d. $ - 2,987

6. Which of the following formulas is used to calculate revenue forecast?
    a. Sales this year/sales last year
    b. Sales last year/sales this year
    c. Sales last year x (1 + % increase estimate)
    d. Sales this year x (1 + % increase estimate)

7. What is the formula for calculating average sales per guest forecast?
   a. Revenue forecast - guest count forecast
   b. Revenue forecast/guest count forecast
   c. Guest count forecast x revenue forecast
   d. Guest count forecast/revenue forecast

8. Which of the following is the formula for calculating guest count forecast?
   a. Guest count last year – guest count this year
   b. Guest count this year x (guest count last year + % increase estimate)
   c. Guest count last year + (guest count last year x % increase estimate)
   d. Guest count last year/guest count this year

9. What is the formula for average sales per guest?
   a. Number of guests served/total revenue
   b. Total revenue x number of guests served
   c. Total revenue - number of guests served
   d. Total revenue/number of guests served

10. Which of the following is *not* the percentage variance formula?
    a. Sales last year/sales this year
    b. Sales this year – sales last year/sales last year
    c. (Sales this year/sales last year) – 1
    d. Variance/sales last year

11. Calculate revenue forecast given the following information: sales last year $120,200; % increase estimate 10%.
    a. $132,220
    b. $108,180
    c. $ 12,020
    d. $ 13,222

12. Calculate guest count forecast given the following information: guests last year 12,500; % increase estimate 5%.
    a.   625
    b. 13,125
    c. 11,875
    d. 18,750

Chapter Answers to Key Terms & Concepts Review, Discussion Questions, and Quiz Yourself

Key Terms & Concepts Review

1. c	5. l	9. d	13. j
2. k	6. a	10. m	14. f
3. e	7. g	11. i	
4. h	8. n	12. b	

Discussion Questions

1. List and explain what the two major types of averages a foodservice manager may encounter and what their formulas are to solve them.
   - Fixed average - The average amount of sales or volume over a specific series or time period, for example, first month of the year or second week of the second month. Formula – Total revenue/number of days
   - Rolling average - The average amount of sales or volume over a changing time period, for example, the last ten days or the last three weeks. Formula – Revenue of days/number of days

2. List three different types of information that may be used for maintaining sales histories.
   - Revenue
   - Number of guests served
   - Average sales per guest
   - Particular menu item served
   - Number of guests served in a specific meal or time period
   - Method of meal delivery

3. Determine what three parts may be involved in predicting future sales.
   - Future revenues
   - Guest counts
   - Average sales per guest levels

4. Determine five advantages that are involved with sales forecasts.
   - Accurate revenue estimates
   - Improved ability to predict expenses
   - Greater efficiency in scheduling needed workers
   - Greater efficiency in scheduling menu item production schedules
   - Better accuracy in purchasing the correct amount of food for immediate use
   - Improved ability to maintain proper levels of nonperishable food inventories
   - Improved budgeting ability

5. List two examples of green practices that can help build customer and employee loyalty, as well as boost profits of foodservice operations.
   - Implementing sustainable practices that focus on conservation
   - Utilizing organic, seasonal, and locally grown products

Quiz Yourself

1. a	7. b
2. c	8. c
3. b	9. d
4. d	10. a
5. a	11. a
6. c	12. b

Chapter 3

Managing the Cost of Food

Learning Outcomes

At the conclusion of this chapter, you will be able to:

- Use sales histories and standardized recipes to determine the amount of food products to buy in anticipation of forecasted sales.

- Purchase, receive, and store food products in a cost-effective manner.

- Compute the cost of food sold and food cost percentage.

Study Notes

1. Menu Item Forecasting

- The menu determines the success of most foodservice operations. Part of this success comes from being able to answer the questions "How many people will I serve today?" and "What will they order?"

- Once you know the average number of people selecting a given menu item, and the total number of guests who made the selections, you can compute the **popularity index**, which is defined as the percentage of total guests choosing a given menu item from a list of alternatives.

> **Popularity Index = Total Number of a Specific Menu Item Sold**
> **Total Number of All Menu Items Sold**

- The basic formula for individual menu item forecasting, based on an item's individual sales history, is as follows:

> **Number of Guests Expected x Item Popularity Index**
> **= Predicted Number of That Item to Be Sold**

- The **predicted number to be sold** is simply the quantity of a specific menu item likely to be sold given an estimate of the total number of guests expected.

- A variety of factors such as competition, weather, special events in your area, facility occupancy, your own promotions, your competitor's promotions, quality of service, and operational consistency come together to influence the number of guests you can expect to serve on any specific day.

- Remember that sales histories track only the general trends of an operation. They are not able to estimate precisely the number of guests who may arrive on any given day.

- Forecasting is crucial if you are to effectively manage your food expenses. Consistency in food production and guest service will greatly influence your overall success.

2. Standardized Recipes

- The **standardized recipe** controls both the quantity and quality of what the kitchen will produce. It details the procedures to be used in preparing and serving each of your menu items.

- Good standardized recipes contain the following information:

  1. Menu item name
  2. Total yield (number of servings)
  3. Portion size
  4. Ingredient list
  5. Preparation/method section
  6. Cooking time and temperature
  7. Special instructions, if necessary
  8. Recipe cost (optional)

- The following list contains arguments often used against standardized recipes:

  1. They take too long to use.
  2. My people don't need recipes; they know how we do things here.
  3. My chef refuses to reveal his or her secrets.
  4. They take too long to write up.
  5. We tried them but lost some, so we stopped using them.
  6. They are too hard to read, or many of my people cannot read English.

- Reasons for incorporating a system of standardized recipes include:

  1. Accurate purchasing is impossible without the existence and use of standardized recipes.
  2. Dietary concerns require some foodservice operators to know exactly the kinds of ingredients and the correct amount of nutrients in each serving of a menu item.
  3. Accuracy in menu laws requires that food service operators be able to tell guests about the type and amount of ingredients in their recipes.
  4. Accurate recipe costing and menu pricing is impossible without standardized recipes.
  5. Matching food used to cash sales is impossible to do without standardized recipes.
  6. New employees can be better trained with standardized recipes.
  7. The computerization of a foodservice operation is impossible unless the elements of standardized recipes are in place; thus, the advantages of advanced technological tools available to the operation are restricted or even eliminated.

- Standardized recipes are the cornerstones of any serious effort to produce consistent, high quality food products at an established cost. Any recipe can be standardized.

- When adjusting recipes for quantity (total yield), two general methods may be employed. They are:

  1. Factor Method
  2. Percentage Technique

- When using the factor method, you utilize the following formula to arrive at a recipe conversion factor:

$$\frac{\text{Yield Desired}}{\text{Current Yield}} = \text{Conversion Factor}$$

- The percentage method deals with recipe weight, rather than with a conversion factor. It is sometimes more accurate than using a conversion factor alone. The proper conversion of weights and measures is important in recipe expansion or reduction.

- The percentage method of recipe conversion is as follows:

$$\text{Ingredient Weight / Total Recipe Weight = \% of Total}$$

Then

$$\text{\% of Total x Total Amount Required} = \text{New Recipe Amount}$$

3. Inventory Control

- A desired inventory level is simply the answer to the question, "How much of each needed ingredient should I have on hand at any one time?"

- **Working stock** is the amount of an ingredient you anticipate using before purchasing that item again.

- **Safety stock** is the extra amount of that ingredient you decide to keep on hand to meet higher than anticipated demand.

- Inventory levels are determined by a variety of factors such as:
  1. Storage capacity
  2. Item perishability
  3. Vendor delivery schedule
  4. Potential savings from increased purchase size
  5. Operating calendar
  6. Relative importance of stock outages
  7. Value of inventory dollars to the operator

- Operators must be careful not to overload storage capacity. Increased inventory of items generally leads to greater spoilage and loss due to theft.

- **Shelf life** is the amount of time a food item retains its maximum freshness, flavor, and quality while in storage. The shelf life of food products varies greatly.

- The cost to the vendor for frequent deliveries will be reflected in the cost of the goods to the operator.

31

- Sometimes you will find that you can realize substantial savings by purchasing needed items in large quantities, and thus receive a lower price from your vendor. There are costs associated with extraordinarily large purchases. These may include: storage costs, spoilage, deterioration, insect or rodent infestation or theft. The operating calendar plays a large part in determining desired inventory levels.

- Some operators over-buy or "stockpile" inventory causing too many dollars to be tied up in non-interest-bearing food products. When this is done, managers incur **opportunity costs.** An opportunity cost is the cost of foregoing the next best alternative when making a decision.

- A state institution that is given its entire annual budget at the start of its **fiscal year** (a year that is 12 months long but may not follow the calendar year) may find it advantageous to use its purchasing power to acquire large amounts of inventory at the beginning of the year and at very low prices.

- A **purchase point**, as it relates to inventory levels, is simply that point in time when an item should be reordered. This point is typically designated by one of two methods:

    1. As needed (just in time)
    2. Par level

- When you elect to use the **as needed**, or **just in time** method of determining inventory levels, you are basically purchasing food based on your prediction of unit sales and the sum of the ingredients (from standardized recipes) necessary to produce those sales.

- Foodservice operators may set predetermined purchase points, called **par levels**, for some items. When determining par levels, you must establish both minimum and maximum amounts required.

- As a rule, highly perishable items should be ordered on an as-needed basis, while items with a longer shelf life can often have their inventory levels set using a par level system.

4. Purchasing

- Purchasing is essentially a matter of determining the following:

    1. What should be purchased?
    2. What is the best price to pay?
    3. How can a steady supply be assured?

- A **product specification (spec)** is simply a detailed description of an ingredient or menu item. A spec is a way for you to communicate in a very precise way with a vendor so that your operation receives the *exact* item requested every time.

- Each menu item or ingredient should have its own spec.

- A foodservice specification generally consists of the following information:

  1. Product name or specification number
  2. Pricing unit
  3. Standard or grade
  4. Weight range/size
  5. Processing and/or packaging
  6. Container size
  7. Intended use
  8. Other information such as product yield

- The exact product name is important when writing specs. When developing the product specification, you may find it helpful to assign a number to the item as well as its name. This can be useful when, for example, many forms of the same ingredient or menu item may be purchased.

- The product name must be specific enough to clearly and precisely identify the item you wish to buy.

- A pricing unit may be established in terms of pounds, quarts, gallons, cases, or any other commonly used unit.

- Many food items are sold with varying degrees of quality or desirability. Because that is true, the U.S. Department of Agriculture, Bureau of Fisheries, and the Food and Drug Administration have developed standards for many food items.

- Weight range or size is important when referring to meats, fish, poultry, and some vegetables. **Count,** in the hospitality industry, is a term that is used to designate size.

- Processing and/or packaging refer to the product's state when you buy it. Also, the labor cost of washing, trimming, and otherwise preparing fresh products, must be considered when comparing their price to that of a canned or frozen product.

- "Farm to Fork" refers to the path food follows from those who grow or raise it, to those who will prepare and serve it. Ideally, this path would be short, to maximize freshness, minimize health risks and be environmentally friendly. For that reason many foodservice operators prefer to seek out and buy locally grown foods whenever possible.

- In addition to their freshness, locally grown foods are good for the environment because their lessened storing, shipping and packaging requirements mean they require less energy to transport and generate less solid waste from excessive packing materials. Reduced transportation and packaging costs often translate into lower prices charged to foodservice operators.

- Container size refers to the can size, number of cans per case, or weight of the container in which the product is delivered. An operator should spec container size.

- Different types of the same item are often used in the same foodservice operation, but in a variety of ways. That is why managers should spec the intended use of each product.

- Additional information such as product yield may be included in a specification if it helps the vendor understand exactly what you have in mind when your order is placed. **Product yield** is simply the amount of product that you will have remaining after cooking, trimming, portioning, or cleaning.

- The **best price** is more accurately stated as the lowest price that meets the long-term goals of both the foodservice operation and its vendor.

- The vehicle used to engage in comparison-shopping among vendors is called the **bid sheet.**

- After you have received bids from your suppliers, you can compare those bids on a **Price comparison sheet.**

- Bid sheets and price comparison sheets may be used to determine the specific vendor who can supply the lowest price, but they do not give enough information to determine the best price.

- Even with the use of product specifications, vendor dependability, quality of vendor service, and accuracy in delivery can be determining factors when attempting to determine the "best price."

- Buying strictly from the price comparison sheet may result in orders too small to meet a supplier's **minimum order requirement**, that is, the smallest order that can be placed with a vendor who delivers. If the minimum order requirement cannot be met using the lowest prices, then the manager may have to choose the supplier with the next highest price to fill a complete order.

- Your food salesperson can be one of your most important allies in controlling costs. Suppliers have a variety of prices based on the customer to whom they are quoting them.

- It is simply in the best interest of a supplier to give a better price to a high volume customer.

- **Cherry Pickers** is the term used by the suppliers to describe the customer who gets bids from multiple vendors, then buys only those items each vendor has "on sale" or for the lowest price.

- Operators who are slow to pay will find that the vendor has decided to add the extra cost of carrying their account to the price the operator pays for his or her products.

- Vendors can be a great source of information related to new products, cooking techniques, trends, and alternative product usage.

- Using one or perhaps two primary vendors tends to bring the average delivery size up, and should result in lower per-item prices. On the other hand, giving one vendor all of the operation's business can be dangerous and costly if the items to be purchased vary widely in quality and price.

- Staples and non-perishables are best purchased in bulk from one vendor. Orders for meats, produce, and some bakery products are best split among several vendors, perhaps with a primary and secondary vendor in each category so that you have a second alternative should the need arise.

- **Ethics** have been defined as the choices of proper conduct made by an individual in his or her relationships with others.

- Ethics come into play in purchasing products because of the tendency for some suppliers to seek an unfair advantage over the competition by providing "personal" favors to the buyer.

- A **daily inventory sheet** will have the items listed in your storage areas, their unit of purchase, and their par values pre-printed on the sheet. In addition, the form will have the following columns: on-hand, special order, and order amount.

- The par value is listed so that you know how much inventory you *should* have in storage at any given time.

- The amount to be ordered is calculated as follows:

> **Par Value – On-Hand x Special Order = Order Amount**

- Regardless of your communication method, it is critical that you prepare a written **purchase order**, or record of what you have decided to buy. The purchase order (PO) should be made out in triplicate (3 copies).

- The written Purchase Order form should contain space for the following information:

  Purchase Order Information
  1. Item Name
  2. Spec #, if appropriate
  3. Quantity Ordered
  4. Quoted Price Per Unit
  5. Extension Price
  6. Total Price of Order
  7. Vendor Information
  8. Purchase Order Number
  9. Date Ordered
  10. Delivery Date
  11. Name of person who placed order
  12. Name of person who received order
  13. Delivery Instructions
  14. Comments

- The advantages of a written Purchase Order are many and include the following:

  1. Written verification of quoted price
  2. Written verification of quantity ordered
  3. Written verification of the receipt of all goods ordered
  4. Written and special instructions to the receiving clerk, as needed
  5. Written verification of conformance to product specification
  6. Written authorization to prepare vendor invoice for payment

5. Receiving

- It is wise for you to establish the purchasing and receiving functions so that one individual places the order, while another individual is responsible for verifying delivery and acceptance of the product.

- **Auditors** are individuals responsible for reviewing and evaluating proper operational procedures. They can determine the potential for fraud or theft.

- If it is not possible to have more than one person involved in the buying process, the work of the purchasing agent/receiving clerk must be carefully monitored by management to prevent fraud.

- Proper receiving demands:

    1. Proper location
    2. Proper tools and equipment
    3. Proper delivery schedules
    4. Proper training

- The receiving area must be large enough to allow for checking products delivered against both the delivery invoice (the seller's record) and the PO (the buyer's record).

- Accessibility to equipment required to move products to their proper storage area and to dispose of excess packaging is important. Make sure the area stays free of trash and clutter, as these make it too easy to hide delivered food items.

- Remember that the delivery person is also a potential thief.

- The receiving area should be kept extremely clean, since you do not want to contaminate incoming food, or provide a carrying vehicle for pests. The area should be well lit and properly ventilated.

- Receiving clerks should have the following equipment: scales, wheeled equipment, box cutter, thermometer, calculator, and records area.

- Scales should be of two types; those accurate to the fraction of a pound, and those accurate to the fraction of an ounce.

- Some operators demand that deliveries be made only at certain times; these are called **acceptance hours**.

- **Refusal hours** are the times that operators will not accept deliveries.

- Receiving clerks should be trained to verify the following product characteristics: weight, quantity, quality, and price.

- Receiving clerks should be required to weigh all meat, fish, and poultry delivered, with the exception of unopened Cryovac (sealed) packages.

- When an item is ordered by weight, it should be verified by weight.

- The counting of boxes, cases, barrels, etc. should be routine. The counting of individual items in a box, such as lemons should be done periodically, but the value of counting on a regular basis is questionable.

- No area is of greater concern to the operator than that of the appropriate quality of product delivered. Checking for quality means checking the entire shipment for conformance to specifications.

- In cases when the vendor is out of the spec item, clerks must know whether it is management's preference to accept a product of higher quality, lower quality, or no product as a substitute.

- Clerks need to be trained in two areas regarding pricing: matching PO unit price to invoice unit price, and verifying price extensions and total.

- When the person responsible for purchasing food places an order, the confirmed quoted price should be recorded on the PO.

- When a discrepancy is discovered, management should be notified immediately. The ethical manager is not happy with either an over-charge or an under-charge situation.

- If management notification is not possible, both the driver and the receiving clerk should initial the "Comment" section of the PO, showing the difference in the two prices.

- **Shorting** is the term used in the industry to indicate that an ordered item has not been delivered as promised.

- A **credit memo** is simply a formal way of notifying the vendor that an item listed on the original invoice is missing, and thus the value of that item should be deducted from the invoice total.

- Some operators deal with suppliers in such a way that a contract price is established. A **contract price** is simply an agreement between buyer and seller to hold the price of a product constant over a defined period of time.

- **Extended price** is simply the unit price multiplied by the number of units delivered.

- Never assume extensions are correct because a computer did them!

- If a supplier consistently shorts your operation, that supplier is suspect both in terms of honesty and lack of concern for your operation's long-term success.

- Training your receiving clerk to assess and evaluate quality products is a continuous process.

- Some large operations use a receiving record when receiving food.

- A receiving record generally contains the following information: name of supplier, invoice number, item description, unit price, number of units delivered, total cost, storage area, and date of activity.

- Receiving reports can be helpful if it is important to record where items are to be delivered, or have been delivered.

Part 2

6. Storage

- Remember that storage costs money, in terms of the space for items, and the money that is tied up in inventory items.

- In most establishments, the storage process consists of four parts: placing products in storage, maintaining product quality and safety, maintaining product security, and determining inventory value.

- Most often, in foodservice, the high perishability dictates that the same person responsible for receiving the items is the person responsible for their storage.

- The two storage methods used are LIFO and FIFO.

- When using the **LIFO** (last in, first out) method, the store-room operator intends to use the most recently delivered product before he or she uses any part of that same product previously on hand.

- **FIFO** (first in, first out) means that the operator intends to rotate stock in such a way that product already on hand is sold prior to the sale of more recently delivered products.

- FIFO is the preferred storage technique for most perishable and non-perishable items. Failure to implement a FIFO system of storage management can result in excessive product loss due to spoilage, shrinkage, and deterioration of quality.

- Some foodservice managers require the storeroom clerk to mark or tag each delivered item with the date of delivery.

- Some operators prefer to go even further when labeling some products for storage. These operators date the item and then also indicate the day (or hour) in which the product should be pulled from storage, thawed, or even discarded.

- Products are generally placed in one of three major storage areas: dry storage, refrigerated storage, or frozen storage.

- Dry storage areas should generally be maintained at a temperature ranging between 65 and 75°F (18 and 24°C).

- Shelving must be sturdy, easy to clean, and at least 6 inches above the ground to allow for proper cleaning beneath the shelving and to ensure proper ventilation.

- Dry goods should never be stored directly on the floor. Labels should face out for easy identification.

- Refrigerator temperatures should generally be maintained between 32°F (0°C) and 36°F (2°C). Refrigerators actually work by removing heat from the contents, rather than "making" food cold.

- Refrigerators should have easily cleaned shelving units that are at least six inches off the floor and are slotted to allow for good air circulation.

- Freezer temperatures should be maintained between 0°F and –10°F (–18°C and –23°C). What is usually called a freezer, however, is more properly a "frozen food storage unit."

- Frozen food holding units must be regularly maintained, a process that includes cleaning inside and out, and constant temperature monitoring to detect possible improper operation.

- Regardless of the storage type, food and related products should be stored neatly in some logical order.

- Food product quality rarely improves with increased storage time.

- The primary method for ensuring the quality of stored products is through proper product rotation and high standards of storeroom sanitation.

- Storage areas are excellent breeding grounds for insects, some bacteria, and also rodents. To protect against these hazards, you should insist on a regular cleaning of all storage areas.

- Refrigerators and frozen-food holding units remove significant amounts of stored product moisture, causing shrinkage in meats and produce and **freezer burn.** Freezer burn refers to deterioration in product quality resulting from poorly wrapped or stored items kept at freezing temperatures.

- Both refrigerators and frozen food holding units should be kept six to ten inches from walls to allow for the free circulation of air around, and efficient operation of, the units.

- Drainage systems in refrigerators should be checked at least weekly.

- In larger storage areas, hallways should be kept clear and empty of storage materials or boxes.

- Some employee theft is impossible to detect. Even the most sophisticated, computerized control system is not able to determine if an employee or vendor's employee walked into the produce walk-in and ate one green grape.

- Make it difficult to remove significant amounts of food from storage without authorization.

- Most foodservice operators attempt to control access to the location of stored products.

- It is your responsibility to see to it that the storeroom clerk maintains good habits in securing product inventory.

- As a general rule, if storerooms are to be locked, only one individual should have access during any shift.

- It is not possible to know your actual food expense without an accurate inventory.

- **Issuing** is the process of placing of products into the production system.

- Valuing, or establishing a dollar value for your entire inventory is achieved by using the following inventory value formula:

$$\boxed{\textbf{Item Amount x Item Value = Item Inventory Value}}$$

- Item amount may be determined by counting the item, as in the case of cans, or by weighing items, as in the case of meats.

- If inventory amounts are overstated, or **padded inventory**, costs will appear artificially low until the proper inventory values are determined.

- Either the LIFO or FIFO method determines item value.

- When the LIFO method is used, the item's value is said to be the price paid for the least recent (oldest) addition to item amount.

- If the FIFO method is used, the item value is said to be the price paid for the most recent (newest) product on hand.

- FIFO is the more common method for valuing foodservice inventory.

- Inventory value is determined using a form similar to the **inventory valuation sheet** shown in Figure 3.22. The inventory valuation sheet should be completed each time the inventory is counted. It can be manually prepared or produced as part of an inventory evaluation software program.

- It is recommended that one person takes the actual physical inventory, and a different person extends the value of that inventory.

- A **physical inventory**, one in which the food products are actually counted, must be taken to determine your actual food usage.

7. Determining Actual Food Expense

- **Cost of food sold** is the dollar amount of all food actually sold, thrown away, wasted or stolen. It is computed as follows:

> **Beginning Inventory**
> **PLUS**
> **Purchases**
> **= Goods Available for Sale**
> **LESS**
> **Ending Inventory**
> **= Cost of Food Consumed**
> **LESS**
> **Employee Meals**
> **= Cost of Food Sold**

- **Beginning inventory** is the dollar value of all food on hand at the beginning of the accounting period.

- **Purchases** are the sum cost of all food purchased during the accounting period.

- **Goods available for sale** is the sum of the beginning inventory and purchases.

- **Ending inventory** refers to the dollar value of all food on hand at the end of the accounting period.

- **Cost of food consumed** is the actual dollar value of all food used, or consumed, by the operation.

- **Employee meal** cost is actually a labor-related, *not* food-related cost. Free or reduced-cost employee meals are a benefit much in the same manner as medical insurance or paid vacation.

- It is important to note that ending inventory for one accounting period becomes the beginning inventory figure for the next period.

- Food or beverage products may be transferred from one food service unit to another. For example, it is likely that fruits, juices, vegetables, and similar items are taken from the kitchen for use in the bar, while wine, sherry, and similar items may be taken from the bar for use in the kitchen.

- Transfers out of the kitchen are subtracted from the cost of food sold and transfers in to the kitchen are added to the cost of food sold.

- A foodservice operation's cost of food consumed is affected by a variety of factors. One such factor relates to the "source reduction" decisions made by the operation's suppliers. Where recycling occurs within the foodservice operation and seeks to reuse materials, "source reduction" is utilized by suppliers to minimize the amount of resources initially required to package, store and ship the items they sell. The result of effective source reduction is a lessened impact on the environment and lower product costs.

- Food cost percentage is both the traditional way of looking at food expense and generally the method used by most operators when preparing the profit and loss statement.

- The formula used to compute actual food cost percentage is as follows:

$$\frac{\text{Cost of Food Sold}}{\text{Food Sales}} = \text{Food Cost \%}$$

- **Food Cost %** represents that portion of food sales that was spent on food expenses.

- The physical inventory may be taken as often as desired to estimate the daily cost of food sold.

- Figure 3.26 illustrates a six-column form, which you can use for a variety of purposes. One of them is to estimate food cost % on a daily or weekly basis.

Six Column Food Cost % Estimate

1. $\dfrac{\text{Purchases Today}}{\text{Sales Today}} = \text{Cost \% Today}$

2. $\dfrac{\text{Purchases to Date}}{\text{Sales to Date}} = \text{Cost \% to Date}$

8. Technology Tools

- This chapter focused on managing food-related costs by controlling the areas of purchasing, receiving, storage, and issuing. There are a variety of software programs that are available that can assist in these areas such as:

    1. Recipe Software can maintain and cost standardized recipes as well as maintain and supply dietary information by portion.
    2. Menu Programs can create and print physical menus and even produce purchase orders based on selected menus.
    3. Purchasing Software can compare bids and make purchase recommendations based on best cost/best value.
    4. Receiving Software can prepare a daily receiving report and maintain receiving histories.
    5. Storage/Inventory Assessment Programs can maintain product inventory values by food category and even compute LIFO or FIFO inventory values.
    6. Cost of Goods Sold Programs can compare forecasted to actual cost of goods sold as well as maintain employee meal records.

- Perhaps it is in the area of managing food products, from their purchase to usage, that you can most effectively utilize the rapidly advancing technological tools available today.

Key Terms & Concepts Review

Match the key terms with their correct definitions.

1. Popularity index _____

2. Predicted number to be sold _____

3. Standardized recipe _____

4. Recipe ready _____

5. Working stock _____

6. Safety stock _____

7. Carryovers _____

8. Shelf life _____

9. Opportunity cost _____

10. Fiscal year _____

11. Purchase point _____

12. As needed/just in time _____

a. The lowest price that meets the requirement of both the foodservice operation and its vendor.

b. A form used in an inventory control system in which an actual or physical count and valuation of all inventory on hand is taken at the close of each accounting period.

c. The quantity of goods from inventory reasonably expected to be used between deliveries.

d. The hours of the day in which an operation is willing to accept food and beverage deliveries.

e. The point in time when an item held in inventory reaches a level that indicates it should be reordered.

f. The portion of food sales that was spent on food expenses.

g. The choices of proper conduct made by an individual in his or her relationships with others.

h. The price per unit multiplied by the number of units. This refers to a total unit price on a delivery slip or invoice.

i. The percentage of total guests choosing a given menu item from a list of menu alternatives.

j. The sum cost of all food purchased during the accounting period. Determined by adding all properly tabulated invoices for the accounting period.

k. A menu item prepared for sale during a meal period but carried over for use in a different meal period.

l. When food or beverage products are supplied from storage by management for use in an operation.

13. Par level _____

14. Product specification/spec _____

15. Count _____

16. Product yield _____

17. Best price _____

18. Bid sheet _____

19. Price comparison sheet _____

20. Minimum order requirement _____

21. Cherry picker _____

22. Ethics _____

m. A detailed description of an ingredient or menu item.

n. The dollar value of all products on hand at the end of the accounting period. This amount is determined by completing a physical inventory.

o. The procedures to be used for consistently preparing and serving a given menu item.

p. A listing of products requested by the purchasing agent. The purchase order lists various product information, including quantity ordered and price quoted by the vendor.

q. A listing of several vendors' bid prices on selected items that results in the selection of a vendor, based on the best price.

r. With the first-in, first-out method of storage, the operator intends to sell his or her oldest product before selling the most recently delivered product.

s. A method of determining the number of a given menu item that is likely to be sold if the total number of customers to be served is known.

t. An addendum to the vendor's delivery slip (invoice) that reconciles differences between the delivery slip and the purchase order.

u. A form that lists the items in storage, the unit of purchase, and the par value. It also contains the following columns: on hand, special order, and order amount.

v. The dollar amount of all food actually sold, thrown away, wasted or stolen plus or minus transfers from other units, minus employee meals.

23. Daily inventory sheet _____

w. These are additions to par stock, held as a hedge against the possibility of extra demand for a given product. This helps reduce the risk of being out of stock on a given item.

24. Purchase order _____

x. Those individuals responsible for reviewing and evaluating proper operational procedures.

25. Auditors _____

y. A customer who buys only those items from a supplier that are the lowest in price among the supplier's competition.

26. Acceptance hours _____

z. When the vendor is unable to deliver the quantity of item ordered for the appropriate delivery date.

27. Refusal hours _____

aa. A recipe ingredient that is cleaned, trimmed, cooked, and generally completed, save for its addition to the recipe.

28. Shorting _____

bb. Free or reduced-cost meals that are employee benefits and are labor-related, not food-related, costs.

29. Credit memo _____

cc. Start and stop dates for a 365-day accounting period. This period need not begin in January and end in December.

30. Contract price _____

dd. The sum of the beginning inventory and purchases. It represents the value of all food that was available for sale during the accounting period.

31. Extended price _____

ee. The smallest order, usually expressed in dollar value, that can be placed with a vendor who delivers.

32. LIFO _____

ff. The term used to describe the inappropriate activity of adding a value for non-existing inventory items to the value of total inventory in an effort to understate actual costs.

33. FIFO _____

gg. Term used to designate size. Size as established by number of items per pound or number of items per container.

34. Freezer burn	_____	hh.	The dollar value of all products on hand at the beginning of the accounting period. This amount is determined by completing a physical inventory.
35. Issue	_____	ii.	The amount of product remaining after cooking, trimming, portioning, or cleaning.
36. Padded inventory	_____	jj.	Those hours of the day in which an operation refuses to accept food and beverage deliveries.
37. Inventory valuation sheet	_____	kk.	A form used to compare prices among many vendors in order to select the best prices.
38. Physical inventory	_____	ll.	A price mutually agreed upon by supplier and operator. This price is the amount to be paid for a product or products over a prescribed period of time.
39. Cost of food sold	_____	mm.	The cost of foregoing the next best alternative when making a decision. For example, with two choices, A & B, both having potential benefits or returns, if A is chosen, then the potential benefits from choosing B are lost.
40. Beginning inventory	_____	nn.	With the last-in, first-out method of storage, the operator intends to sell his or her most recently delivered product before selling the older product.
41. Purchases	_____	oo.	A system of determining purchase point by using sales forecasts and standardized recipes to decide how much of an item to place in inventory.
42. Goods available for sale	_____	pp.	The actual dollar value of all food used, or consumed, by the operation.
43. Ending inventory	_____	qq.	The period of time an ingredient or menu item maintains its freshness, flavor, and quality.
44. Cost of food consumed	_____	rr.	The process of documenting all inventory items, the quantity on hand, and the unit value of each item.

45. Employee meal cost	_____	ss.	A system of determining purchase point by using management-established minimum and maximum allowable inventory levels for a given inventory item.
46. Source reduction	_____	tt.	Deterioration in product quality resulting from poorly wrapped or stored items at freezing temperatures.
47. Food cost %	_____	uu.	Techniques used by food manufacturers and wholesalers to reduce product packaging waste.

Discussion Questions

1. Determine what two methods can be used to adjust recipes for quantity.

_____

_____

_____

_____

2. When purchasing items what three questions must be determined?

_____

_____

_____

_____

3. List and explain the four most important features of receiving inventory.

_____

_____

_____

_____

4. List and explain the three types of storage areas.

_____

_____

_____

_____

5. Explain how a foodservice operation's cost of food consumed is affected by source reduction.

_____

_____

_____

_____

Quiz Yourself

Choose the letter of the best answer to the questions listed below.

Questions 1 and 2 are based on the following information:

Menu Item	Number Sold	Popularity Index	Forecast # Guests	Forecast Item Sold
Pork Chops	145			
Pot Roast Dinner	275			
Chicken Pot Pie	380			
Total			1000	

1. What is the popularity index for the Pork Chops and Chicken Pot Pie?
    a. 0.2500, 0.5000
    b. 0.3524, 0.1724
    c. 0.4624, 0.1965
    d. 0.1813, 0.4750

2. What is the number of forecasted Pot Roast Dinners? (Round up answer to the nearest whole number.)
    a. 344
    b. 270
    c. 350
    d. 205

3. Calculate the cost of food sold based on the following information: beginning inventory $15,000; purchases $6,000; employee meals $1,000; ending inventory $8,000.
    a.   9,000
    b. 15,000
    c. 12,000
    d.   8,000

4. Calculate order amount: par value 10, on hand 3, special order 4.
    a.   9
    b. 10
    c. 15
    d. 11

5. Calculate cost of food consumed: beginning inventory $6,000; purchases $8,000; ending inventory $4,500; employee meals $1,000.
    a. $ 9,500
    b. $ 8,500
    c. $18,500
    d. $10,000

6. Which of the following formulas is used for computing conversion factor?
   a. Current yield/yield desired
   b. Ingredient weight/total recipe weight
   c. Yield desired/current yield
   d. Total recipe weight/ingredient weight

7. What is the formula for calculating item inventory value?
   a. Item value + item amount
   b. Item value/item amount
   c. Item amount x item value
   d. Item amount - item value

8. Which of the following formulas is used to calculate extended price?
   a. Unit price + number of items delivered
   b. Unit price x number of items delivered
   c. Unit price/number of items delivered
   d. Number of items delivered - unit price

9. What is the formula for calculating cost % today?
   a. Purchases today/sales today
   b. Purchases today x purchases to date
   c. Purchases to date x sales today
   d. Sales today/purchases to date

10. What is the formula for calculating cost % to date?
    a. Purchases today x purchases to date
    b. Purchases to date x sales today
    c. Sales today/purchases to date
    d. Purchases to date/sales to date

11. Calculate food cost % based on the following information: cost of food sold $15,000; food sales $46,000.
    a. 32.61%
    b. 0.32%
    c. 30.66%
    d. 3.06%

12. Tom Brown is a chef. His current recipe makes 70 cupcakes. He wishes to make 150 cupcakes. What is the conversion factor?
    a. 0.46
    b. 2.14
    c. 4.60
    d. 0.21

Chapter Answers to Key Terms & Concepts Review, Discussion Questions, and Quiz Yourself

Key Terms & Concepts Review

1. i	11. e	21. y	31. h	41. j
2. s	12. oo	22. g	32. nn	42. dd
3. o	13. ss	23. u	33. r	43. n
4. aa	14. m	24. p	34. tt	44. pp
5. c	15. gg	25. x	35. l	45. bb
6. w	16. ii	26. d	36. ff	46. uu
7. k	17. a	27. jj	37. rr	47. f
8. qq	18. kk	28. z	38. b	
9. mm	19. q	29. t	39. v	
10. cc	20. ee	30. ll	40. hh	

Discussion Questions

1. Determine what two methods can be used to adjust recipes for quantity.
   - Factor Method – Changes the number of portions in a recipe to the number of portions desired
   - Percentage Technique – Deals with recipe weight rather than conversions. This technique is sometimes more accurate.

2. When purchasing items what three questions must be determined?
   - What should be purchased?
   - What is the best price to pay?
   - How can a steady supply be assured?

3. List and explain the four most important features of receiving inventory.
   - Proper Location – The "back door" is usually where all the receiving is done. The receiving area must be adequate to handle the job of receiving, or product loss and inconsistency will result.
   - Proper Tools and Equipment – Some items are standard in any receiving operation, such as the following:
     - Scales
     - Wheeled equipment
     - Box cutter
     - Thermometer
     - Calculator
     - Records area

- Proper Delivery Schedules – Scheduling should be during slow periods, were there would be plenty of time for a thorough checking of the products delivered.
- Proper Training – Receiving clerks should be properly trained to verify the following product characteristics:
  - Weight
  - Quantity
  - Quality
  - Price

4. List and explain the three types of storage areas.
- Dry storage – These areas should generally be maintained at a temperature ranging between 65 and 75°F (between 18 and 24°C).
- Refrigerated storage – These areas should generally be maintained between 32 and 36°F (between 0 and 2°C).
- Freezer storage – These areas should be maintained between 0 and –10°F (between –18 and –23°C).

5. Explain how a foodservice operation's cost of food consumed is affected by source reduction.
- Source reduction is utilized by suppliers to minimize the amount of resources initially required to package, store and ship the items they sell. The result of effective source reduction is a lessened impact on the environment and lower product costs.

Quiz Yourself

1. d	7. c
2. a	8. b
3. c	9. a
4. d	10. d
5. a	11. a
6. c	12. b

Chapter 4

Managing the Cost of Beverages

Learning Outcomes

At the conclusion of this chapter, you will be able to:

- Use sales histories and standardized drink recipes to develop a beverage purchase order.

- Compute the dollar value of bar transfers both to and from the kitchen.

- Compute an accurate cost of goods sold percentage for beer, wine, and spirits.

Study Notes

1. Serving Alcoholic Beverages

- **Alcoholic beverages** are those products that are meant for consumption as a beverage, and that contain a significant amount of ethyl alcohol.

- Alcoholic beverages are generally classified as beer, wine, or spirits.

- **Beer** is a fermented beverage made from grain and flavored with hops.

- **Wine** is a fermented beverage made from grapes, fruits, or berries.

- **Spirits** are fermented beverages that are distilled to increase the alcohol content of the product.

- These products will be specified, ordered, received, and stored much like food products. However, there are control issues that are much more difficult to handle.

- Such controls must be modified to meet the characteristic and inherent increased responsibility created by the sale of alcoholic beverages.

- There are two primary classifications of establishments that serve alcohol: restaurants that use it as an accompaniment to food, and those locations whose primary offering is alcohol.

- In moderate doses, ethyl alcohol is a mild tranquilizer; in excessive doses, it can become toxic.

- While the special requirements involved in serving alcoholic beverages are many, the control of beverage costs is similar to that of food-related costs.

- **Dramshop laws**, passed in many states, shift the liability for acts committed by an individual under the influence of alcohol from that individual to the server or operation that supplied the intoxicating beverage.

- In all states, the sale of alcoholic beverages is regulated either by the licensing of establishments that are allowed to sell alcoholic beverages **(license states)** or by direct control and sale of the products by the state **(control states)**.

2. Forecasting Beverage Sales

- Due to the limitless possibilities, forecasting customer item selection is difficult.

- Forecasting beer sales is basically the same as forecasting any regular menu item. By using sales histories, operators can determine what percentage of their customers will order beer, and which kind of beer and in what packaging format they will prefer their beer.

- **Keg beer** is also known as **draft beer**, or beer in a form of packaging in which the beer is shipped to you in multi-gallon units for bulk sale.

- Forecasting wine sales is divided into two parts: forecasting bottled-wine sales and forecasting wine-by-the-glass sales.

- When forecasting sales by the bottle, treat a bottled wine just like an individual menu item.

- While bottled wine is not highly perishable, all wine products are perishable to some degree; thus, excessive inventory of some wine types can result in increased product loss through oxidation (deterioration) and/or theft.

- Generally, forecasting the sale of **house wines**, includes those wines served to a guest who does not stipulate a specific brand when ordering, as well as those named wines offered by the glass.

- While the number of guests who order a mixed drink can be tracked, the exact item the guests request is very difficult to determine.

- One method categorizes all drinks based on the spirit that forms the base of the drink.

- Spirit sales can also be tracked by generic product name, specific product name, or specific drink requested.

- Obviously, different methods have varying degrees of accuracy. Operators must decide which is best for their establishment based on the cost effectiveness involved.

3. Standardized Drink Recipes and Portions

- Control is more important at the bar than in the kitchen because the potential for waste and employee theft is greater.

- However, it is still unrealistic to expect a bartender to consult a standardized recipe for every drink.

- Operators should remember: beverage operations are subject to tax audits, beverage operations can be closed down for violations, employees may bring in their own products to sell and keep sales revenue, and detecting the disappearance of small amounts of beverage products is very difficult.

- The following is the beverage cost % formula:

$$\frac{\text{Cost of Beverage Sold}}{\text{Beverage Sales}} = \text{Beverage Cost \%}$$

- While standardized recipes (including step-by-step prep methods) may only be necessary for a few types of drinks, standardized recipes that detail the quantity of beverage product predetermined by management as appropriate should be strictly adhered to.

- To insure that liquor is poured accurately, a **jigger**, a tool for measuring liquid, or an automated device programmed to dispense these predetermined amounts should be used.

- A standardized recipe sheet should be prepared for each drink item for costing purposes.

4. Purchasing Beverage Products

- While food products only require one level of quality per item, several levels of quality are chosen for alcoholic beverages.

- Beer is the most highly perishable of beverage products, with a **pull date**, or expiration date of only a few months. Operators must, therefore, carefully select brand and packaging methods.

- Generally, geographic location, clientele, ambiance, and menu help determine what beer product will be selected.

- Bartenders should maintain a beer **product request log** so that guest requests that cannot be filled are noted and monitored by management.

- Beer is typically sold in cans, bottles, or kegs.

- Draft beer (beer from kegs) is often the preferred choice and cheaper for operators to serve. However, special equipment and serving techniques are required.

- The shelf life of keg beer is the shortest of all packaging types, ranging from 30 to 45 days for an untapped keg, that is, one that has not yet been opened by the bartender, and even fewer days for a **tapped** (opened) keg.

- Wine must also be selected according to product and packaging.

- Operators generally sell wine by the glass, bottle, and split or half bottle.

- If wine is also purchased for cooking, it will be bought from the beverage wholesaler also, but generally not of the same quality as that purchased for drinking.

- As a good manager, you will build a **wine list**—the term used to describe your menu of wine offerings—that fits your own particular operation and guest expectations.

- In developing a **wine list**, operators must offer choices for guests who want to spend a lot or a little.

- A **vintner** is a wine producer.

- Wines that either complement the food or, in the case of a bar, are popular with the guests must be available.

- However, avoid the temptation to offer too many wines on a wine list.

- Wait staff should be trained to be knowledgeable but not intimidating to guests.

- Generally, if operators are having trouble selling wine, the difficulty lies in the delivery of the product rather than with the product selected.

- Distilled spirits have an extremely long shelf life; therefore, a wrong purchase is not usually a disaster.

- While packaging is not a major concern of the operator selecting a spirit product, brand quality is crucial.

- In general, operators will select spirits in two major categories, well and call liquors.

- **Well liquors** are those spirits that are poured when the customer does not specify a particular brand name when ordering.

- **Call liquors** are those requested by brand name; extremely expensive call liquors are sometimes referred to as **premium liquors**.

- Operators generally charge a higher price for call or **premium liquors**.

- Remember, guests who order well liquors may be price conscious, but that does not mean they are not quality conscious also.

- Quality spirit products at fair prices build customer loyalty.

- Depending on the state and county, special laws may influence how beverage purchases are to be made or paid for.

- The goal in purchasing beverages is to have an adequate, but not excessive, amount of product on hand at all times.

- Available organic spirits products include Vodka, Gin, Tequila, Scotch and Rum. While more expensive than non-organic versions of the same product, these items are increasingly available for purchase from main-line beverage distributors. Organic wines and beers are also becoming increasingly common.

- Concerns about costs can plague green beverage initiatives because organic product costs are historically higher, and in the past, the number of interested customers has been smaller. Today, however, using seasonal and local produce and juices for drink production can help moderate every operation's costs while increasing quality.

- A **broken case** occurs when several different brands or products are used to completely fill the case.

- As a general rule, wine, beer, and spirits are purchased by the case.

5. Receiving Beverage Products

- Since beverage products do not vary in quality, as does food, skill required to receive beverages is somewhat less than what is needed for receiving food.

- As with food, the receiving clerk needs a proper location, tools, and equipment.

- Proper delivery schedules must be maintained.

- When matching the purchase order to the vendor invoice, only quantity ordered and price must be verified.

- If beer is **fresh dated**, that is, a date is stamped on the product to indicate its freshness, very little inspection is required to ensure that the product is exactly what was ordered.

- Key beverage receiving checkpoints are: correct brand, correct bottle size, no broken bottles, freshness dates (beer), correct vintage (wine), correct unit price, correct price extension, and correct invoice total.

- If errors are detected, a credit memo should be filled out and signed by both the delivery person and the receiving clerk.

- A credit memo is an addendum to the vendor's delivery invoice that reconciles differences between the purchase order and the delivery invoice.

6. Storing Beverage Products

- Storage areas should be clean, free of infestation, and large enough to allow for easy rotation of stock.

- Security is crucial. A **two-key system** is often used to control access to beverage storage areas. The individual responsible for the beverage area has one key while the other key is kept in a sealed envelope in a secured area. In the event of emergency, the envelope can be opened.

- Spirits should be stored in a relatively dry storage area between 70 and 80°F (21 to 27°C).

- Beer in kegs or unpasteurized containers should be stored at refrigeration temperatures of 36 to 38°F (2 to 3°C).

- Canned beer should be covered when stored to eliminate the chance of dust or dirt settling on the rims of the cans.

- Pasteurized beer should be stored in a cool dark room at 50 to 70°F (10 to 21°C).

- Product rotation is critical if beer is to be served at its maximum freshness.

- The three components critical to wine storage are temperature, light, and cork condition.

- Generally, wines should be stored at a temperature of 50 to 65°F (10 to 18°C).

- Heat is an enemy of effective wine storage.

- When storing wine, it should be exposed only to the minimum amount of light necessary.

- The cork protects wine from its greatest enemy, oxygen. **Oxidation** occurs when oxygen comes in contact with bottled wine; you can detect a wine that has been overly oxidized because it smells somewhat like vinegar. Oxidation deteriorates the quality of bottled wines.

- Wine should always be stored in such a way, usually on its side, so that the cork remains in contact with the wine to stay moist.

- Storage should keep the cork, and thus the wine, cool, dark and moist.

7. Bar Transfers

- The great majority of product cost related to bar operations is alcoholic beverages.

- As far as spirits are concerned, nonalcoholic food products may be served as a part of the drink order and must be transferred from the kitchen to bar.

- If transfers are not controlled and recorded, the restaurant's food cost percentage will be artificially inflated while the total beverage cost percentage in the bar will be understated.

- Likewise, bar items may be used in the kitchen and must also be properly noted.

- The control procedure for kitchen and bar transfers is actually quite simple, requiring only consistency.

8. Computing Cost of Beverages

- When computing the beverage cost percentage, there is only one difference from computing the food cost percentage; there is no equivalent for "employee meals" since employees should not be drinking.

Beginning Inventory
PLUS
Purchases
      = **Goods Available for Sale**
LESS
Ending Inventory
LESS
Transfers from Bar
PLUS
Transfers to Bar
      = **Cost of Beverage Sold**

---

9. Special Features of Liquor Inventory

- Unopened containers of beer, wine, and spirits can, of course, be counted. Opened containers, however, must be valued also. Three inventory methods are commonly in use to accomplish this goal. They are:

  1. Weight
  2. Count
  3. Measure

10. Sales Mix

- **Sales mix** is defined as the series of guest purchasing decisions that result in a specific food or beverage cost percentage.

- Guests can contribute to major changes in the food or beverage cost percentages, due to sales mix.

- To analyze the beverage sales mix, the item % of total beverage sales must be calculated, as follows:

Item Dollar Sales
Total Beverage Sales = **Item % of Total Beverage Sales**

---

11. Technology Tools

- For those operations that sell a significant amount of alcoholic beverage products, there are a variety of programs designed to discourage theft and carefully monitor product sales and expenses.

- In fact, the software and hardware available to help you in the beverage service area is generally more sophisticated than that found in most food-related areas.

- Programs available in the beverage area include those that can help you:
  1. Monitor product sales.
  2. Monitor product (inventory) usage.
  3. Calculate actual and targeted pour percentages.
  4. Adjust product costs for happy hours and specials, as well as product transfers to and from the kitchen.
  5. Maintain adequate levels of product inventory.
  6. Establish par stock quantities and values.
  7. Generate purchase orders.
  8. Schedule employees based on forecasted sales levels.
  9. Create and print customized wine lists and specials menus.
  10. Maintain sales histories.
  11. Maintain drink recipe files.
  12. Project the impact of sales mix on beverage cost percentages.

- It is important to realize that some bar-related software may be dependent on specific and sometimes expensive automated beverage dispensing systems.

- Other software is either stand-alone or designed to operate in conjunction with many of the basic POS systems currently on the market.

Key Terms & Concepts Review

Match the key terms with their correct definitions.

1. Alcoholic beverages _____

   a. A record of guest beverage requests that are not currently available.

2. Beer _____

   b. A system to control access to storage areas.

3. Wine _____

   c. A menu of wine offerings.

4. Spirits _____

   d. A process which occurs when oxygen comes in contact with bottled wine, resulting in a deterioration of the wine product.

5. Dramshop laws _____

   e. Those spirits that are served by an operation when the customer does not specify a particular brand name.

6. Blood alcohol content (BAC) _____

   f. A measure of the level of alcohol existing in the blood of a person who has been drinking alcoholic beverages. Each state sets its own allowable limit of BAC for establishing intoxication of motor vehicle drivers.

7. License states _____

   g. A locking system that allows management to issue multiple keys and to identify precisely the time an issued key was used to access the lock, as well as to whom that key was issued.

8. Control states _____

   h. Term used to identify beer products sold in a keg.

9. Percent selecting _____

   i. A case of beverage products in which several different brands or products make up the contents of the case.

10. Keg beer/draft beer _____

   j. Those products that are meant for consumption as a beverage and that contain a significant amount of ethyl alcohol. They are classified as beer, wine, or spirits.

11. House wine	_____	k.	The series of consumer purchasing decisions that result in a specific food and beverage cost percentage. Sales mix affects overall product cost percentage any time menu items have varying food and beverage cost percentages.
12. Jigger	_____	l.	States that regulate the sale of alcoholic beverages by direct control and sale of the products by the state.
13. Pull date	_____	m.	A food package upon which a date is stamped to indicate the freshness of its contents.
14. Product request log	_____	n.	A fermented beverage made from grain and flavored with hops.
15. Tapped keg	_____	o.	Expensive call liquors.
16. Wine list	_____	p.	The term used to describe a series of legislative acts that, under certain conditions, holds businesses and, in some cases, individuals, personally responsible for the actions of guests who consume excessive amounts of alcoholic beverages. These "laws" shift the liability for acts committed by an individual under the influence of alcohol from that individual to the server or operation that supplied the intoxicating beverage.
17. Vintner	_____	q.	A draft beer container (keg) that has been opened.
18. Well liquors	_____	r.	States that regulate the sale of alcoholic beverages by the licensing of establishments.
19. Call liquors	_____	s.	A bar device used to measure predetermined quantities of alcoholic beverages. Jiggers usually are marked in ounces and portions of an ounce, for example, 1 ounce or 1 1/2 ounces.
20. Premium liquors	_____	t.	Fermented beverages that are distilled to increase the alcohol content of the product.

21. Broken case	_____	u.	A fermented beverage made from grapes, fruits, or berries.
22. Fresh dated	_____	v.	A bottle of wine that is approximately one-half the size of the standard 750-milliliter wine bottle. Typically sold for either room service or dining room consumption.
23. Two-key system	_____	w.	A formula for determining the proportion of people who will buy a given menu item from a list of menu choices.
24. Recodable electronic locks	_____	x.	The term used to indicate the type of wine to be served in the event a specific brand name product is not requested by the guest.
25. Half-bottle or split	_____	y.	Wine Producer.
26. Oxidation	_____	z.	Those spirits that are requested (called for) by a particular brand name.
27. Sales mix	_____	aa.	Expiration date on beverage products, usually beers, after which they should not be sold.

Discussion Questions

1. List the 5 of the 9 Key Beverage Receiving Checkpoints that a manager would check when receiving beverage products.

   _____
   _____
   _____
   _____

2. List and explain the three different types of alcoholic beverages.

   _____
   _____
   _____
   _____

3. Explain liquor, beer, and wine storage procedures and their temperatures.

_____

_____

_____

_____

4. Identify and explain the three inventory methods for open beverage containers.

_____

_____

_____

_____

5. Identify organic beverages that are increasingly available for purchase from main-line beverage distributors and explain how to decrease the operation's cost of organic beverages.

_____

_____

_____

_____

Quiz Yourself

Choose the letter of the best answer to the questions listed below.

1. Calculate the cost of beverage sold by using the following information: beginning inventory $9,000; purchases $5,000; ending inventory $3,000; transfers from bar $1,500; transfers to bar $1,100.
   a. $12,400
   b. $ 9,300
   c. $10,600
   d. $ 8,900

2. Calculate item % of total beverage sales using the following information: total beverage sales $15,000; item dollar sales $6,000.
   a. 40.0%
   b. 2.5%
   c. 25.0%
   d. 45.0%

3. Calculate beverage cost % using the following information: cost of beverage sold $5,400; beverage sales $11,300 (round to the nearest whole percent).
   a. 27%
   b. 65%
   c. 12%
   d. 48%

4. Calculate % banquet beer sales using the following information: beer sales $25,000; total beverage sales $75,000.
   a. 38%
   b. 33%
   c. 68%
   d. 29%

5. Calculate food cost % and beverage cost % given the following: beverage costs $35,600; food costs $ 52,250; beverage sales $210,000; food sales $195,000; total sales $405,000 (round to the nearest whole percent).
   a. Food cost % = 38% ; beverage cost % = 22%
   b. Food cost % = 43% ; beverage cost % = 48%
   c. Food cost % = 27% ; beverage cost % = 17%
   d. Food cost % = 19% ; beverage cost % = 35%

6. Which of the following is the formula for computing cost of beverage sold?
   a. Beginning inventory + purchases – ending inventory – transfer from bar + transfers to bar.
   b. Beginning inventory + ending inventory – purchases + transfer from bar – transfers to bar.
   c. Ending inventory – beginning inventory + purchases - transfers to bar + transfers from bar
   d. Beginning inventory + purchases – ending inventory - transfer to bar + transfer from bar.

7. Which of the following formulas are used for computing item % of total beverage sales?
   a. Item dollar sales - total beverage sales
   b. Item dollar sales x total beverage sales
   c. Total beverage sales/item dollar sales
   d. Item dollar sales/total beverage sales

8. What is the formula for computing beverage cost %?
   a. Total sales/beverage sales
   b. Cost of beverage sold/beverage sales
   c. Beverage sales/total sales
   d. Beverage sales/cost of beverages sold

9. Which of the following is the formula for computing % banquet wine sales?
   a. Banquet wine sales x total banquet beverage sales
   b. Total banquet beverage sales - banquet wine sales
   c. Banquet wine sales - total banquet beverage sales
   d. Banquet wine sales/total banquet beverage sales

10. Which of the following formulas is *not* correct for calculating cost of beverage sold (assuming no transfers)?
    a. Beginning inventory + purchases - ending inventory
    b. Beginning inventory - purchases + ending inventory
    c. Beginning inventory + purchases – ending inventory – employee meals
    d. All of the above
    e. Only b. and c. above

11. Calculate the cost of beverage sold by using the following information: beginning inventory $15,000; purchases $10,000; ending inventory $12,000; transfers from bar $3,500; transfers to bar $2,100; employee meals $1,500.
    a. $11,600
    b. $14,400
    c. $10,100
    d. $14,100

12. Calculate food cost % and beverage cost % given the following: beverage costs $24,600; food costs $ 42,250; beverage sales $190,000; food sales $175,000; total sales $365,000 (round to the nearest whole percent).
   a. Food cost % = 30% ; beverage cost % = 13%
   b. Food cost % = 24% ; beverage cost % = 13%
   c. Food cost % = 27% ; beverage cost % = 17%
   d. Food cost % = 12% ; beverage cost % = 35%

Chapter Answers to Key Terms & Concepts Review, Discussion Questions, and Quiz Yourself

Key Terms & Concepts Review

1. j	6. f	11. x	16. c	21. i	26. d
2. n	7. r	12. s	17. y	22. m	27. k
3. u	8. l	13. aa	18. e	23. b	
4. t	9. w	14. a	19. z	24. g	
5. p	10. h	15. q	20. o	25. v	

Discussion Questions

1. List the 5 of the 9 Key Beverage Receiving Checkpoints that a manager would check when receiving beverage products.
    *   Correct brand
    *   Correct bottle size
    *   No broken bottles or bottle seals
    *   Freshness dates (beer)
    *   Correct vintage, or year produced (wine)
    *   Refrigerated state (if appropriate)
    *   Correct unit price
    *   Correct price extension
    *   Correct invoice total

2. List and explain the three different types of alcoholic beverages.
    *   Beer – A fermented beverage made from grain and flavored with hops
    *   Wine – A fermented beverage made from grapes, fruits, or berries
    *   Spirits – Fermented beverages that are distilled to increase the alcohol content of the product

3. Explain liquor, beer, and wine storage procedures and their temperatures.
    *   Liquor storage – Spirits should be stored in a relatively dry storage area between 70 and 80°F (21 to 27°C).
    Beer storage – Beer in kegs should be stored at refrigeration temperatures of 36 to 38°F (2 to 3°C) because keg beer is unpasteurized and, thus, must be handled carefully to avoid excessive bacteria. Product rotation is critical if beer is to be served at its maximum freshness.

- Wine storage – Wine storage is the most complex and time consuming activity required of beverage storeroom personnel. For proper wine storage to be sufficient, three factors have to be achieved.
  - Temperature
  - Light
  - Cork condition

4. Identify and explain the three inventory methods for open beverage containers.
   - Weight – The weight method uses a scale to weigh open bottles of liquor. The system is effective if you remember to subtract the weight of the empty bottle itself from the total product weight.
   - Count – Counting full bottles is easy, counting the value of partial bottles is more difficult. If the tenths system is used, the inventory taker assigns a value of 10/10 to a full bottle and 5/10 to a half bottle and so on. When inventory is taken, the partial bottle is examined and the appropriate tenth is assigned based on the amount left in the bottle.
   - Measure - Some beverage managers determine product levels of open bottles by using a ruler to determine the amount the bottle contains. Dollar values are then assigned to each inch or portion of an inch for inventory evaluation purposes. This method has a high degree of accuracy and is favored by many.

5. Identify organic beverages that are increasingly available for purchase from main-line beverage distributors and explain how to decrease the operation's cost of organic beverages.
   - Available organic spirits products include vodka, gin, tequila, scotch and rum. Organic wines and beers are also becoming increasingly common.
   - Using seasonal and local produce and juices for drink production can help moderate every operation's costs while increasing quality.

Quiz Yourself

1. c	7. d
2. a	8. b
3. d	9. d
4. b	10. e
5. c	11. a
6. a	12. b

Chapter 5

Managing the Food and Beverage Production Process

Learning Outcomes

At the conclusion of this chapter, you will be able to:

- Use management techniques to control the costs of preparing food and beverages for guests.

- Compute the actual cost of producing a menu item and compare that cost against the cost you planned to achieve.

- Recognize and be able to apply various methods to reduce the cost of goods sold percentage.

Study Notes

1. Managing the Food and Beverage Production Process

- The most important function of management is controlling the food and beverage production process.

- Fundamentally, each foodservice manager is in charge of kitchen production.

- Planning daily production schedules is important because you will want to have both the products and staff needed to properly service your guests.

- Ideally, the process of determining how much of each menu item to prepare on a given day would look as follows:

> **Prior Day's Carryover + Today's Production**
> **= Today's Sales Forecast +/– Margin of Error**

- Regardless of the type of operation you manage, you will likely find that some of your menu items simply do not retain their quality well when they are carried over.

73

- Some foodservice managers pre-print their production sheets listing all menu items and thus ensure that production levels for each major menu item are considered on a daily basis. Others prefer to use the production sheet on an "as needed" basis.

- When your kitchen production staff knows what you want them to produce for a given meal period, they can move to the next logical step which is to **requisition**, or request, the inventory items they must have to produce the menu items indicated on your production schedule.

- These inventory items are then **issued,** that is, taken from storage and placed into the food and beverage production areas.

2. Product Issuing

- Often, foodservice managers create difficulties for their workers by developing a requisition system that is far too time-consuming and complicated.

- The difficulty in such an approach usually arises because management hopes to equate products *issued* with products *sold* without taking a physical inventory.

- Maintaining product security can be achieved if a few principles are observed:

    1. Food, beverages, and supplies should be requisitioned only as needed based on approved production schedules.
    2. Required items (issues) should be issued only with management approval.
    3. If a written record of issues is to be kept, each person removing food, beverages, or supplies from the storage area must sign, acknowledging receipt of the products.
    4. Products that do not ultimately get used should be returned to the storage area, and their return recorded.

- Some larger operators who employ a full-time storeroom person prefer to operate with advance requisition schedules.

- Sometimes products are even weighed and measured for kitchen personnel; here, the storeroom is often called an **ingredient room**.

- The total cost is arrived at by computing the value of the issued amount, not the requisitioned amount.

- It is vital that a copy of the storeroom requisition form be sent to the purchasing agent after it has been prepared so that this individual will know about the movement of products in and out of the storage areas.

- The basic principles of product issuing which apply to food and supplies also apply to beverages.

- Beverage issues are generally one of two types: liquor storeroom issues, wine cellar issues.

- The **empty for full system** of liquor replacement requires bartenders to hold empty liquor bottles in a bar or a closely adjacent area; at a designated time each empty liquor bottle is replaced with a full one.

- All liquor issued from the liquor storage area should be marked or stamped in such a manner that is not easily duplicated.

- The issuing of wine from a wine cellar is a special case of product issuing because these sales cannot be predicted as accurately as sales of other alcoholic beverage products.

- If the wine storage area contains products valuable enough to remain locked, it is reasonable to assume that each bottled wine issued should be noted.

- In the case of transfers to the kitchen or the bar, it should be noted that the product has been directed to one of these two locations rather than having been assigned to a guest transaction number (maintained by the POS system) or a guest check number (when using a manual system).

- In an issues system, the dollar amount of issues is used to form the basis of the estimate.

- The six-column form requires only that the manager divide today's issues by today's sales to arrive at the today estimate as follows:

$$\frac{\text{Issues Today}}{\text{Sales Today}} = \textbf{Beverage Cost Estimate Today}$$

- The "to date" columns represent cumulative totals of both issues and sales. Therefore, add today's issues to the issues total of the prior day and do the same with the sales figures to calculate the beverage cost estimate to date as follows:

$$\frac{\text{Issues to Date}}{\text{Sales to Date}} = \textbf{Beverage Cost Estimate to Date}$$

- These estimates will be extremely close to the actual cost of goods sold percentage if bar inventory remains constant or nearly constant in total dollar value from month to month.

- Adjust issues back to actual inventory levels at the end of the accounting period. If ending inventory is lower than beginning inventory, the difference between the two numbers is *added* to the issues total. If ending inventory is higher than beginning inventory, the difference in these two numbers will be *subtracted* from the issues total. Cost of beverage sold can be computed as follows:

$$\frac{\text{Issues to Date} + \text{Inventory Adjustment}}{\text{Sales to Date}} = \text{Cost of Beverage Sold}$$

- Inventory levels can vary based on delivery days of vendors, the day of the week inventory is taken, and even the seasonality of some businesses. Because of this variability, it is critical that you perform the month-end inventory adjustment.

3. Inventory Control

- Regardless of the methods used by employees to requisition food and beverage products, or management to issue these, inventory levels will be affected. It will be your responsibility and that of your purchasing agent to monitor this movement and purchase additional products, as needed.

- Restocking the inventory is critical if product shortages are to be avoided and if product necessary for menu item preparation is to be available.

- A **physical inventory** is one in which an actual, physical count and valuation of all inventory on hand is taken at the close of each accounting period.

- A **perpetual inventory** system is one in which the entire inventory is counted and recorded, then additions to and deletions from total inventory are recorded as they occur.

- The physical inventory, if properly taken, is the most accurate of all, since each item is actually counted and then valued.

- The perpetual inventory is especially popular in the area of liquor and wine.

- A **bin card** is simply an index card (or line on a spreadsheet) that details additions to and deletions from a given product's inventory level.

- **Perpetual inventory cards** are simply bin cards, but they include the product's price. A new perpetual inventory card or spreadsheet line is created each time the product's purchase price changes, with the quantity of product on hand entered on the new card.

- In the foodservice industry, it is not wise to depend exclusively on a perpetual inventory system.

- The ABC inventory system was designed to combine both the physical and perpetual inventory systems. It separates inventory items into three main categories:

  1. Category A items are those that require tight control and the most accurate record keeping. Those are typically high-value items, and while few in number, they can make up 70% to 80% of the total inventory value.

  2. Category B items are those that make up 10% to 15% of the inventory value and require only routine control and record keeping.

  3. Category C items make up only 5% to 10% of the inventory value. These items require only the simplest of inventory control systems.

- To develop the A, B, and C categories, you simply follow these steps.

  1. Calculate monthly usage in units (pounds, gallons, cases, etc.) for each inventory item.

  2. Multiply total unit usage times purchase price to arrive at the total monthly dollar value of product usage.

  3. Rank items from highest dollar usage to lowest.

- It is not necessary that the line between A, B, and C products be drawn at any given point. A common guideline is:

  Category A, top 20% of items
  Category B, next 30% of items
  Category C, next 50% of items

- It is important to note that while the percentage of items in category A is small, the percentage of total monthly product cost the items account for is large. Conversely, while the number of items in category C is large, the total dollar value of product cost the items account for is small.

- The ABC inventory system attempts to direct management's attention to the areas where it is most needed, especially of high cost.

- Regardless of the inventory system used, management must be strict in monitoring both withdrawals from inventory and the process by which inventory is replenished.
- You compute your **category food cost %**, that is, a food cost percentage computed on a portion of total food usage, by using the cost of food sold/sales formula.

The proportion of total cost percentages is developed by the formula:

$$\frac{\text{Cost in Product Category}}{\text{Total Cost in All Categories}} = \text{Proportion of Total Product Cost}$$

4. Managing the Food Production Area

- Often, those individuals who manage restaurants do so because they relish managing the **back of the house**, or kitchen production area, of the food facility.

- Managing the food production process entails control of the following five areas: waste, overcooking, overserving, improper carryover utilization, and inappropriate make or buy decisions.

- Food losses through simple product waste can play a large role in overall excessive cost situations.

- In general, it can be said that food waste is the result of poor training or management inattentiveness.

- Increased cooking time or temperature can cause product shrinkage that increases average portion cost.

- To control loss due to overcooking, management must strictly enforce standardized recipe cooking times.

- Overportioning has the effect of increasing operational costs, and may cause the operation to mismatch its production schedule with anticipated demand.

- Overportioning must also be avoided because guests want to feel that they have received fair value for their money. Consistency is a key to operational success in foodservice.

- In most cases, tools are available that will help employees serve the proper portion size.

- Management should have a clear use in mind for each menu item that may have to be carried over, and those items should be noted on production schedules so they don't get stored and lost in freezers or refrigerators.

- It is important to understand that **carryover** foods seldom can be sold for their original value.

- Nearly all foodservice operations today use food products that are prepared in some fashion, called **convenience** or **ready foods**.

- Convenience or ready foods can save dollars spent on labor, equipment, and hard-to-secure food products to your operations. However, these items tend to cost more on a per-portion basis.

- In general, the following guidelines may be of value when determining whether to adopt the use of a convenience product.

    1. Is the quality acceptable?
    2. Will the product save labor?
    3. Would it matter if the guest knew?
    4. Does the product come in an acceptable package size?
    5. Is storage space adequate?

5. Managing the Beverage Production Area

- Controlling the amount of the product that actually is served to the guest is more complex with alcoholic beverages than with food.

- In its simplest, but least desired form, beverage production can consist of a bartender **free-pouring,** which is, pouring liquor from a bottle without carefully measuring the poured amount. In a situation such as this, it is very difficult to control product costs.

- Unlike food production, the beverage manager has a greater choice in automated equipment to help with controls.

- A **jigger** is a device (like a small cup) used to measure alcoholic beverages, typically in ounces, and fraction of ounce quantities.

- In some situations, you may determine that a **metered bottle** or other metered dispensing unit makes sense. In this case, a predetermined portion of product is dispensed whenever the bartender is called upon to serve that product.

- In some large operations, beverage "guns" are connected directly to liquor products. The gun may be activated by pushing a mechanical or electronic button built into the gun or POS.

- The most expensive, but also the most complete solution, a **total bar system** combines sales information with product dispensing information to create a complete revenue and product management system.

- Depending on the level of sophistication and cost, the total bar system can perform one or all of the following tasks:

    1. Record beverage sale by brand.
    2. Record who made the sale.
    3. Record sales dollars and/or post the sale to a guestroom folio (bill) in a hotel.
    4. Measure liquor.
    5. Add predetermined mixes to drink.
    6. Reduce liquor from inventory.
    7. Prepare liquor requisition.
    8. Compute liquor cost by brand sold.
    9. Calculate gratuity on check.
    10. Identify payment method, that is, cash, check, credit card.
    11. Record guest sale (check) number.
    12. Record date and time of sale.

- Other issues of beverage production management that should be of concern to the effective beverage manager are in-room mini-bars, bottle sales, open bars, and banquet operations.

- The control issue with mini-bars in hotel rooms is one of matching requests by housekeeping for replenishment bottles with guest usage of product.

- When liquor sales are made by the bottle, either through room service or at a reception area, the control issue is one of verifying bottle count.

- **Open bars** are ones in which no charge is made for the individual drinks at the time they are served.

- The production control issues associated with open bars fall into one of two main categories: portion size and accountability.

- Some managers have virtually eliminated the open bar concept, preferring to go to a coupon system where each coupon issued is good for one drink. This way, the number of coupons issued, rather than the number of drinks, can be controlled.

- With states holding liquor sellers responsible for the actions of their patrons through the enactment of dramshop legislation, the entire concept of reasonable and prudent care in beverage operations is called into question.

- The sale of alcoholic beverages during a banquet usually takes the form of bottled-wine sales.

- If the payment is based on the number of bottles served, the bottles should be marked and the empties made available for inspection by either the guest or the banquet captain.

6. Employee Theft

- Loss of product can happen when control systems do not prevent employee theft.

- Bar theft is one of the most frequent types of thefts in the foodservice industry.

- While it may be impossible to halt all kinds of bar theft, management should check periodically the following areas: order filled but not rung up, bringing in extra product, over – and underpouring, incorrect change making, dilution of product, product theft, and product substitution.

- Proper portion size in the spirits area is ensured through the enforced use of jiggers, metered devices, or other mechanical or electronic equipment. In the case of draft beer, **head size**, that is the amount of foam on top of the glass, directly affects portion size and portion cost and, thus it too must be controlled.

- Since each alcohol product has a particular specific gravity or weight associated with it, you may also check for product dilution through the use of a **hydrometer**, which identifies specific gravity.

- Management should watch the bar area carefully, or enlist the aid of a **spotter**, a professional who will observe the bar operation with an eye toward reporting any unusual or inappropriate behavior by the bartender.

- Theft may also occur in the area of receptions and special events.

- Remember, anytime the same individual is responsible for both the preparation of a product and the collection of money for its sale, the opportunity for theft is greatly increased.

- Most kitchen-related theft deals with the removal of products from the premises, since few kitchen production workers also handle cash.

- The following product security tips are helpful when designing control systems to ensure the safety and security of food (and beverage) products.

81

Product Security Tips

1. Keep all storage areas locked and secure.
2. Issue food only with proper authorization and management approval.
3. Monitor the use of all carryovers.
4. Do not allow food to be prepared unless a guest check or written request precedes the preparation.
5. Maintain an active inventory management system.
6. Ensure that all food received is signed for by the appropriate receiving clerk.
7. Do not pay suppliers for food products without an appropriate and signed invoice.
8. Do not use "petty cash" to pay for food items unless a receipt and the product can be produced.
9. Conduct systematic physical inventories of all level A, B, and C products.
10. Do not allow employees to remove food from the premises without management's specific approval.

7. Determining Actual and Attainable Product Costs

- Knowledge of actual product cost begins with a standardized recipe cost for each menu item.

- The **standardized recipe cost sheet** is a record of the ingredient costs required to produce an item sold by your operation.

- When costing standardized recipes, many foodservice managers prefer to use whole cent figures rather than fractions of a cent.

- **AP** or **As Purchased** state refers to the weight or count of a product, as delivered to the foodservice operator.

- **EP** or **Edible Portion** refers to the weight of a product after it has been cleaned, trimmed, cooked, and portioned.

- A **yield test** is a procedure used for computing your actual EP costs on a product that will experience weight or volume loss in preparation.

- **Waste %** is the percentage of product lost due to cooking, trimming, portioning, or cleaning.

$$\text{Waste \%} = \frac{\text{Product Loss}}{\text{AP Weight}}$$

82

- Once waste % has been determined, it is possible to compute the yield %.

- **Yield %** is the percentage of product you will have remaining after cooking, trimming, portioning, or cleaning.

$$\text{Yield \%} = 1.00 - \text{Waste \%}$$

- If we know the yield % we can compute the A.P. weight needed to yield the appropriate E.P. weight required, by using the following formula:

$$\frac{\text{EP Required}}{\text{Yield \%}} = \text{AP Required}$$

- To check your figures to see if you should use a particular yield % when purchasing an item, you can proceed as follows:

$$\text{EP Required} = \text{AP Required} \times \text{Yield \%}$$

- Good vendors are an excellent source for providing tabled information related to trim and loss rates for standard products they carry.

- Another way to determine net product yield % is to compute it directly using the following formula:

$$\frac{\text{EP Weight}}{\text{AP Weight}} = \text{Product Yield \%}$$

- To compute actual EP cost, use the following formula:

$$\frac{\text{AP Price per Pound}}{\text{Product Yield \%}} = \text{EP Cost (per pound)}$$

- A carbon footprint has been defined as a measure of the impact human activities have on the environment in terms of the amount of greenhouse gases (carbon dioxide) produced.

- Examples of activities in which foodservice operations engage to help reduce their carbon footprint include: buying food products locally, monitoring efficient energy usage regularly, avoiding the sale of bottled waters where the packaging and shipping of these items result in the unnecessary production of carbon dioxide, using cold water for cleaning when practical and sanitary, and reduce, reuse, and recycle.

- If you are to draw reasonable conclusions regarding operational efficiency, you must be able to compare how well you are doing with how well you should be doing.

- This process begins with determining **attainable product cost**. Attainable product cost is defined as that cost of goods sold figure that should be achievable given the product sales mix of a particular operation.

- The formula for the operational efficiency ratio is as follows:

$$\frac{\text{Actual Product Cost}}{\text{Attainable Product Cost}} = \text{Operational Efficiency Ratio}$$

- You would know your attainable food cost percentage through the use of the following formula:

$$\frac{\text{Cost as per Standardized Recipes}}{\text{Total Sales}} = \text{Attainable Product Cost \%}$$

- This cost excludes any losses due to overcooking, over-portioning, waste, theft, etc. Therefore, the attainable food cost is rarely achieved.

- While it is not possible to determine one range of variance acceptability that is appropriate for all food facilities, it is important for you to establish acceptability ranges for your own facility.

8. Reducing Overall Product Cost Percentage

- While we must remember to guard against inappropriate cost cutting, management can find itself in a position where food and beverage production costs must be reduced.

- The food cost percentage equation is deceptively easy to understand. In its simplest form, it can be represented as:

$$\frac{A}{B} = C$$

Where

A = Cost of Goods Sold
B = Sales
C = Cost Percentage

- In general, the rules of algebra say the following things about the A/B = C formula:

    1. If A is unchanged, and B increases, C decreases.
    2. If A is unchanged, and B decreases, C increases.
    3. If A increases at the same proportional rate B increases, C remains unchanged.
    4. If A decreases while B is unchanged, C decreases.
    5. If A increases and B is unchanged, C increases.

- Put into foodservice management terms, these five algebraic statements can be translated, as follows:

    1. If costs can be kept constant but sales increase, the cost percentage goes down.
    2. If costs remain constant but sales decline, the cost percentage increases.
    3. If costs go up at the same rate sales go up, the cost of goods sold percentage will remain unchanged.
    4. If costs can be reduced while sales remain constant, the cost percentage goes down.
    5. If costs increase with no increase in sales, the cost percentage will go up.

- The six approaches to reducing overall product cost percentage are:

Reducing Overall Product Cost Percentage
1. Decrease portion size relative to price.
2. Vary recipe composition.
3. Adjust product quality.
4. Achieve a more favorable sales mix.
5. Ensure that all product purchased is sold.
6. Increase price relative to portion size.

9. Technology Tools

- In the past, restaurants were slow to install working computer terminals and other technological tools in kitchen areas where production staff could easily use them. Increasingly, however, these installations are being made.

- In a professional kitchen, cost control efforts are often shared between management and the production staff. Advanced technology programs available for kitchen production use include those that can help both you and your production staff members:

1. Perform nutrition-related analysis of menu items.
2. Develop production schedules based on forecasted sales.
3. Create product requisition (issues) lists based on forecasted sales.
4. Compute actual versus ideal costs based on product issues.
5. Estimate and compute daily food cost.
6. Maintain physical or perpetual inventory; compute inventory turnover rates.
7. Maintain product usage record.
8. Compare portions served to portions produced to monitor over portioning.
9. Suggest usage for carryover products.
10. Conduct "make versus buy" calculations to optimize employee productivity and minimize costs.

Key Terms & Concepts Review

Match the key terms with their correct definitions.

1. Requisition _____

   a. A bin card that includes the product's price at the top of the card, allowing for continual tracking of the quantity of an item on hand and its price.

2. Issued _____

   b. An individual employed by management for the purpose of inconspicuously observing bartenders and waitstaff in order to detect any fraudulent or policy-violating behavior.

3. Ingredient room _____

   c. The process of supplying food or beverage products from storage by management for use in an operation.

4. Empty for full system _____

   d. This formula is defined as product loss divided by AP weight and refers to product lost in the preparation process.

5. Comp _____

   e. Predetermined portion of product is dispensed whenever the bartender is called upon to serve that product.

6. Physical inventory _____

   f. Short for the word complimentary, which refers to the practice of management giving a product to a guest without a charge. This can be done for a special customer or as a way of making amends for an operational error.

7. Perpetual inventory _____

   g. Cost of goods sold figure that should be achievable given the product sales mix of a particular operation.

8. Bin card _____

   h. A menu item prepared for sale during a meal period but carried over for use in a different meal period.

9. Perpetual inventory card _____

   i. When a food or beverage product is requested from storage by an employee for use in an operation.

10. Category food cost % _____

j. A bar in which no charge for an individual drink is made to the customer, thus establishing an all-you-can-drink environment. Sometimes referred to as a hotel bar.

11. Back of the house _____

k. An inventory control system in which additions to and deletions from total inventory are noted as they occur.

12. Carryovers _____

l. This term refers to the weight or count of a product as delivered to the foodservice operator.

13. Convenience/ready foods _____

m. The bartender is required to retain empty liquor bottles, and then each empty liquor bottle is replaced with a full one at the beginning of the next shift. The empty bottles are then either broken or disposed of, as local beverage law requires.

14. Free-pouring _____

n. A record of the ingredient costs required to produce an item sold by a foodservice operation.

15. Jigger _____

o. An index card with both additions to and deletions from inventory of a given product. To facilitate its use, the card is usually affixed to the shelf that holds the given item. Used in a perpetual inventory system.

16. Metered bottle _____

p. The amount of space on the top of a glass of beer that is made up of foam. Thus, a glass of beer with one inch of foam on its top is said to have a one-inch head.

17. Total bar system _____

q. This formula is defined as 1 minus waste percentage and refers to the amount of product available for use by the operator after all preparation-related losses have been taken into account.

18. Open bar	_____	r.	A bar device used to measure predetermined quantities of alcoholic beverages. Jiggers usually are marked in ounces and portions of an ounce, for example, 1 ounce or 1 1/2 ounces.
19. Head size	_____	s.	A storeroom or section of a storeroom where ingredients are weighed and measured according to standardized recipes, and then delivered to the appropriate kitchen production area.
20. Hydrometer	_____	t.	System that combines sales information with product dispensing information to create a complete revenue and product management system.
21. Spotter	_____	u.	An inventory control system in which an actual or physical count and valuation of all inventory on hand is taken at the close of each accounting period.
22. Standardized recipe cost sheet	_____	v.	Pouring liquor from a bottle without measuring the poured amount.
23. As Purchased (AP)	_____	w.	A food cost percentage computed on a portion of total food usage. Categories include meat, seafood, dairy, produce, and so on.
24. Edible Portion (EP)	_____	x.	The cost of an item after cooking, trimming, portioning, or cleaning. It represents the cost based on product yield.
25. Yield test	_____	y.	This term refers to the weight or count of a product after it has been trimmed, cooked, and portioned.
26. Waste %	_____	z.	An instrument used to measure the specific gravity of a liquid.
27. Yield %	_____	aa.	The kitchen production area of a foodservice establishment.
28. Edible portion cost (EP cost)	_____	bb.	Food products that are pre-prepared in some fashion.

29. Carbon footprint _____ cc. A procedure used to determine actual EP ingredient costs. It is used to help establish actual costs on a product that will experience weight or volume loss in preparation.

30. Attainable product cost _____ dd. A term used to describe a measure of the impact human activities have on the environment in terms of the amount of greenhouse gases (carbon dioxide) produced.

Discussion Questions

1. Identify and explain two special concerns that have to be addressed when issuing beverage products.

_____
_____
_____
_____

2. List and explain five areas that a manager must control in the food production process.

_____
_____
_____
_____

3. List three questions that must be answered when determining actual and attainable product costs.

_____
_____
_____
_____

4. List the six key factors to reducing overall product cost percentage.

_____
_____
_____
_____

5. List five examples of activities in which foodservice operations engage to help reduce their carbon footprint.

_____

_____

_____

_____

Quiz Yourself

Choose the letter of the best answer to the questions listed below.

1. Using the following information and the formula for beverage cost estimate today, compute the following: issues today $2,250; sales today $10,563.
   a.   21%
   b.   469
   c.   45%
   d.   23

2. Calculate cost of beverages estimate using the following information: issues to date $96,000; ending inventory is $45,000 lower than beginning inventory; sales to date $109,000 (Round to the nearest whole percent.)
   a.   129%
   b.   47%
   c.   28%
   d.   72%

3. Using the information provided, calculate meat cost proportion of total cost: ribs $1,468.26; pork chops $2,989.33; chicken tenders $1,631.98; total cost in all categories $ 22,725.31.
   a.   16,635.74
   b.   36%
   c.   2,189.50
   d.   27%

4. Calculate operational efficiency ratio using the following information: actual product cost $2,000; attainable product cost $ 1,200.
   a.   60%
   b.   122%
   c.   167%
   d.   75%

5. Using the following information compute attainable product cost %: total sales $6,249; cost as per standardized recipe $2,169. (Round to the nearest whole percent.)
   a.   35%
   b.   288%
   c.   39%
   d.   151%

6. Which of the following formulas is used to compute product yield %?
   a.   AP price per pound/AP weight
   b.   EP price per pound/EP weight
   c.   AP weight/EP weight
   d.   EP weight/AP weight

7. What formula is used for computing today's sales forecast?
   a. Today's production – carryovers
   b. Prior-day carryover + today's production
   c. Today's production x carryovers
   d. Prior-day carryover/today's production

8. Determine which of the following formulas equals the proportion of total product cost.
   a. Cost in product category/total cost in all categories
   b. Cost in all categories + cost in product category
   c. Cost in product category x total cost in all categories
   d. Total cost in all categories – cost in product category

9. Identify the formula for computing waste %.
   a. EP weight/AP weight
   b. Product loss/EP weight
   c. EP weight/product loss
   d. Product loss/AP weight

10. What is the formula for computing EP required?
    a. Yield %/AP weight
    b. AP required/ EP weight
    c. AP required x yield %
    d. AP required x EP weight

11. Using the following information and the formula for beverage cost estimate today, compute the following: issues today $1,560; sales today $12,500.
    a.   12.50%
    b.   11.20%
    c.   8.25%
    d.   22.45%

12. Calculate cost of beverages sold using the following information: issues to date $6,000; sales to date $19,000; ending inventory is $1,000 higher than beginning inventory. (Round to the nearest whole percent.)
    a. 20%
    b. 26%
    c.   5%
    d. 31%

Chapter Answers to Key Terms & Concepts Review, Discussion Questions, and Quiz Yourself

Key Terms & Concepts Review

1. i	6. u	11. aa	16. e	21. b	26. d
2. c	7. k	12. h	17. t	22. n	27. q
3. s	8. o	13. bb	18. j	23. l	28. x
4. m	9. a	14. v	19. p	24. y	29. dd
5. f	10. w	15. r	20. z	25. cc	30. g

Discussion Questions

1. Identify and explain two special concerns that have to be addressed when issuing beverage products.
   - Liquor storeroom issues – One method for liquor issuing is the empty for full system, which is replacing an empty bottle of liquor with a full bottle.
   - Wine cellar issues - The issuing of wine from a wine cellar is a special case of product issuing because these sales cannot be predicted as accurately as sales of other alcoholic beverage products. If the wine storage area contains products valuable enough to remain locked, it is reasonable to assume that each bottled wine issued should be noted.

2. List and explain five areas that a manager must control in the food production process.
   - Waste – Food losses through simple product waste can play a large role in overall excessive costs. Wastage can be as simple as not using a spatula to get all of the salad dressing out of a jar.
   - Overcooking – It is a truism that prolonged cooking reduces product volume, whether the item cooked is roast beef or vegetable soup.
   - Over-serving – Over portioning on the part of service personnel has the effect of increasing operational costs and may cause the operation to mismatch its production schedule with anticipated demand.
   - Improper carryover utilization – Food that has been prepared and remains unsold at the end of the operational day is called a carryover or leftover. If these carryover items are not handled properly or stored at the right temperature, the product will not have the same quality. Production schedules must note carryover items on a daily basis.
   - Inappropriate make or buy decisions – Products that are already prepared are called convenience or ready foods, and can be of great value to an operation. These items do have a down side because they may cost more on a per-portion basis.

3. List three questions that must be answered when determining actual and attainable product costs.
   - What are our actual product costs?
   - What should our product costs be?
   - How close are we to this attainable goal?

4. List the six key factors to reducing overall product cost percentage.
   - Decrease portion size relative to price
   - Vary recipe composition
   - Adjust product quality
   - Achieve a more favorable sales mix
   - Ensure that all product purchased is sold
   - Increase price relative to portion size

5. List five examples of activities in which foodservice operations engage to help reduce their carbon footprint.
   - Buying food products locally
   - Monitoring efficient energy usage regularly
   - Avoiding the sale of bottled waters where the packaging and shipping of these items result in the unnecessary production of carbon dioxide
   - Using cold water for cleaning when practical and sanitary
   - Reduce, reuse, and recycle

Quiz Yourself

1. a	7. b
2. a	8. a
3. d	9. d
4. c	10. c
5. a	11. a
6. d	12. b

Chapter 6

Managing Food and Beverage Pricing

Learning Outcomes

At the conclusion of this chapter, you will be able to:

- Choose and apply the best menu format to an operation.

- Identify the variables to be considered when establishing menu prices.

- Assign menu prices to menu items based on their cost, popularity, and ultimate profitability.

Study Notes

1. Menu Formats

- Menus are one of the most effective ways manager's can communicate with their guests. Regardless of the choice the business makes, the menu is an excellent opportunity to build impulse sales or to communicate special sales and services the facility has to offer.

- Menus in foodservice establishments generally fall into one of three major categories: standard, daily, or cycle.

- Menu "**tip-ons**," which are smaller menu segments clipped on to more permanent menus, can prove very effective in influencing impulse buying.

- The **standard menu** is printed, displayed, recited by service staff, or otherwise communicated to the guest. The standard menu is fixed day after day.

- Standard menus simplify the ordering process; guests tend to have a good number of choices, and guest preference data can be easily obtained.

- But, standard menus do not utilize carryovers effectively, do not respond quickly to market changes, and do not allow easy seasonal adjustments.

- The **daily menu** changes every day. Management can respond quickly to changes in ingredient or item prices, and can use carryovers. But, planning is more difficult, as is collecting customer data.

- A **cycle menu** is a menu in effect for a specific time period. The length of the cycle refers to the length of time the menu is in effect.

- Typically, cycle menus are repeated on a regular basis.

- Cycle menus are often selected by managers whose guests dine frequently with them on a very regular basis, as a cycle menu provides a systematic means for incorporating variety into the menu.

- Production personnel can be trained to produce a wider variety of foods with a cycle menu than with a standard menu.

- With cycle menus, purchasing is simplified, inventory levels are easy to maintain, and carryovers are easily utilized.

- Regardless of the menu type used, you can generally incorporate minor menu changes on a regular basis. This is accomplished through the offering of daily or weekly **menu specials**, that is, menu items that will appear on the menu as you desire and be removed when they are either consumed or discontinued.

- Daily or weekly menu specials provide variety, low-cost raw ingredients, carryover utilization, or test-market potential for new menu items.

2. Factors Affecting Menu Pricing

- It is important to remember that revenue and price are not synonymous terms.

- **Revenue** means the amount spent by *all guests* while **Price** refers to the amount charged to *one guest*. Total revenue is generated by the following formula:

> **Price x Number Sold = Total Revenue**

- It is a truism that as price increases, the number of items sold will generally decrease.

- Guests demand a good **price/value relationship** when making a purchase.

- The price/value relationship simply reflects guests' view of how much value they are receiving for the price they are paying.

- It may be said that price is significantly affected by all of the following factors:

> **Factors Influencing Menu Price**
> 1. **Local competition**
> 2. **Service levels**
> 3. **Guest type**
> 4. **Product quality**
> 5. **Portion size**
> 6. **Ambience**
> 7. **Meal period**
> 8. **Location**
> 9. **Sales mix**

- Successful foodservice operators spend their time focusing on building guest value in their *own* operation, and not in attempting to mimic the efforts of the competition.

- Guests expect to pay more for the same product when service levels are higher.

- Some guests are simply less price sensitive than others. All guests, however, want value for their money.

- Foodservice operators should select the quality level that best represents their guests' anticipated desire as well as their goals, and then price the products accordingly.

- Portion size plays a large role in determining menu pricing.

- The proper dish size is just as critical as the proper size of scoop or ladle when serving the food.

- For the foodservice operator who provides an attractive ambience, menu prices can be increased. However, excellent product quality with outstanding service goes much further over the long run than do clever restaurant designs.

- In some cases, diners expect to pay more for an item served in the evening than for that same item served at a lunch period. You must exercise caution in this area. Guests should clearly understand *why* a menu item's price changes with the time of day.

- Location can be a major factor in determining price.

- There is no discounting the value of a prime restaurant location, which can influence price; it does not, however, guarantee success.

- Sales mix refers to the specific menu items selected by guests.

- Sales mix will most heavily influence the menu pricing decision, just as guest purchase decisions will influence total product costs.

- **Price blending** refers to the process of pricing products, with very different individual cost percentages, in groups with the intent of achieving a favorable overall cost situation.

- The formula for computing food cost percentage is as follows:

$$\frac{\text{Cost of Food Sold}}{\text{Food Sales}} = \text{Food Cost \%}$$

- This formula can be worded somewhat differently for a single menu item without changing its accuracy. Consider that:

$$\frac{\text{Costs of a Specific Food Item Sold}}{\text{Food Sales of That Item}} = \text{Food Cost \% of That Item}$$

- It is important to understand that the food sales value in the above formula is a synonymous term to the selling price when evaluating the menu price of a single menu item. The principles of algebra allow you to rearrange the formula as follows:

$$\frac{\text{Cost of a Specific Food Item Sold}}{\text{Food Cost \% of That Item}} = \text{Food Sales (Selling Price) of That Item}$$

- The Leadership in Energy and Environmental Design (LEED) rating system developed by the U.S. Green Building Council (USGBC) evaluates facilities on a variety of standards.

- The rating system considers sustainability, water use efficiency, energy usage, air quality, construction and materials, and innovation.

3. Assigning Menu Prices

- In general, menu prices are most often assigned on the basis of one of the following two concepts: product cost percentage or contribution margin.

- The **product cost percentage** is based on the idea that product cost should be a predetermined percentage of selling price.

- When management uses a predetermined food cost percentage to price menu items, it is stating its belief that product cost in relationship to selling price is of great importance.

- A cost factor or multiplier can be assigned to each desired food cost percentage as follows:

$$\frac{1.00}{\text{Desired Product Cost \%}} = \text{Pricing Factor}$$

- The pricing factor when multiplied by any product cost will result in a selling price that yields the product cost. The formula is as follows:

$$\text{Pricing Factor} \times \text{Product Cost} = \text{Menu Price}$$

- A **plate cost** is simply the sum of all product costs included in a single meal (or "plate") served to a guest.

- **Contribution margin** is defined as the amount that remains after the product cost of the menu item is subtracted from the item's selling price. Contribution margin is computed as follows:

$$\text{Selling Price} - \text{Product Cost} = \text{Contribution Margin}$$

- When this approach is used, the formula for determining selling price is:

$$\text{Product Cost} + \text{Contribution Margin Desired} = \text{Selling Price}$$

- The effective manager will view pricing as an important process with an end goal of setting a good price/value relationship in the mind of the guest.

- Regardless of whether the pricing method used is based on food cost percentage or contribution margin, the selling price selected must provide for a predetermined operational profit.

4. Special Pricing Situations

- Some pricing decisions faced by foodservice managers call for a unique approach. In many cases, pricing is used as a way to influence guests' purchasing decisions or to respond to particularly complex situations. The following are examples: coupons, value pricing, bundling, salad bars and buffets, bottled wine, beverages at receptions and parties.

- Coupons are a popular way to vary menu price. There are two types of coupons in use in the hospitality industry. The first type generally allows guests to get a free item anytime they buy another item. With the second type, some form of restriction is placed on the coupon's use.

- Coupons have the effect of reducing sales revenue from each guest in the hope that the total number of guests will increase to the point that total sales revenue increases.

- **Value Pricing** refers to the practice of reducing prices on selected menu items in the belief that, as in couponing, total guest counts will increase to the point that total sales revenue also increases.

- **Bundling** refers to the practice of selecting specific menu items and pricing them as a group in such a manner that the single menu price of the group is lower than if the items in the group were purchased individually.

- When bundling, as in couponing or value pricing, lower menu prices are accepted by management in the belief that this pricing strategy will increase total sales revenue and thus profit, by increasing the number of guests served.

- The difficulty in establishing a set price for either a salad bar or buffet is that total portion cost can vary greatly from one guest to the next.

- The secret to keeping the selling price low in a salad bar or buffet is to apply the ABC inventory approach. That is, A items should comprise no more than 20% of the total product available; B items, no more than 30%; and C items, 50%.

- Use the following formula to determine buffet product cost per guest:

$$\frac{\text{Total Buffet Product Cost}}{\text{Guests Served}} = \text{Buffet Product Cost per Guest}$$

- Few areas of menu pricing create more controversy than that of pricing wines by the bottle. The reason for this may be the incredible variance in cost among different **vintages** or years of production, as well as the quality of alternative wine offerings.

- How you decide to price the bottled wine offerings on your menu will definitely affect your guest's perception of the price/value relationship offered by your operation.

- The **price spread** is defined as the range between the lowest and highest priced menu item.

- Pricing beverages for open-bar events can be difficult, since each consumer group can be expected to behave somewhat differently when attending an open bar or hosted bar function.

- When charging on a per person, per hour basis you must have a good idea of how much the average attendee will consume during the length of the party or reception so that an appropriate price can be established.

- Also, maintaining past events and records of what the average consumption for each group of guests has been previously can help you establish an appropriate price.

5. Technology Tools

- In this chapter you learned about the menu formats you most often encounter as hospitality managers, as well as the factors affecting menu prices, and the procedures used to assign individual menu item prices based on cost and sales data.

- The mathematical computations required to evaluate the effectiveness of individual menu items and to establish their prices can be complex, but there are a wide range of software products available that can help you:

  1. Develop menus and cost recipes.
  2. Design and print menu "specials" for meal periods or happy hours.
  3. Compute and analyze item contribution margin.
  4. Compute and analyze item and overall food cost percentage.
  5. Price banquet menus and bars based on known product costs.
  6. Evaluate the profitability of individual menu items.
  7. Estimate future item demand based on past purchase patterns.
  8. Assign individual menu item prices based on management-supplied parameters.

- Menu analysis and pricing software is often packaged as part of a larger software program. It is an area that will continue to see rapid development in the future as software makers seek additional ways to improve their products.

Key Terms & Concepts Review

Match the key terms with their correct definitions.

1. Tip-on (menu) _____

    a. Menu items that will appear on the menu and be removed when they are either consumed or discontinued. These daily or weekly specials are an effort to provide variety, take advantage of low-cost raw ingredients, utilize carryover products, or test market potential of new menu items.

2. Standard menu _____

    b. The specific year(s) of production for a wine.

3. Daily menu _____

    c. The process of assigning prices based on product groups for the purpose of achieving predetermined cost objectives.

4. Cycle menu _____

    d. A menu that changes every day.

5. Menu specials _____

    e. The practice of reducing all or most prices on the menu in the belief that total guest counts will increase to the point that total sales revenue also increases.

6. Revenue versus price _____

    f. Revenue means the amount spent by *all* guests while price refers to the amount charged to *one* guest.

7. Price/value relationship _____

    g. The difference in price on a menu between the lowest and highest priced item of a similar nature.

8. Price blending _____

    h. A printed and otherwise fixed menu that stays the same day after day.

9. Plate cost _____

    i. The profit or margin that remains after product cost is subtracted from an item's selling price.

10. Contribution margin _____

    j. A menu that is in effect for a predetermined length of time, such as 7 days or 14 days.

11. Value pricing	_____	k.	The practice of selecting specific menu items and pricing them as a group, in such a manner that the single menu price of the group is lower than if the items comprising the group were purchased individually.
12. Bundling	_____	l.	The guests' view of how much value they are receiving for the price they are paying.
13. Vintage	_____	m.	Smaller menu segments intended to influence impulse buying that are attached to more permanent menus.
14. Price spread	_____	n.	The sum of all product costs included in a single meal (or plate) served to a guest.

Discussion Questions

1. Identify and explain the three major menu formats.

_____
_____
_____
_____

2. List the nine factors that influence menu price.

_____
_____
_____
_____

3. List and explain two methods of assigning menu prices.

_____
_____
_____
_____

4. Identify and explain four of the six special pricing situations.

_____

_____

_____

_____

5. List the four ratings of LEED certification, including levels and points.

_____

_____

_____

_____

Quiz Yourself

Choose the letter of the best answer to the questions listed below.

1. Use the following information to calculate food cost % of an item: selling price of an item $11.95; cost of a food item sold $3.75. (Round numbers to the nearest whole percent.)
    a. 35%
    b. 40%
    c. 31%
    d. 15%

2. Using the factor method, determine the sales price given the following: desired product cost % 40%; product cost $1; covers served 400.
    a. Sales price = $6.00
    b. Sales price = $2.50
    c. Sales price = $5.50
    d. Sales price = $8.00

3. Calculate the buffet product cost per guest using the following information: guests served 375; total buffet product cost $1,252; pricing factor 2.000.
    a. $ 3.34
    b. $ 5.51
    c. $10.25
    d. $ 5.99

4. The EP cost of your lamb dinner item is $5.25 and your desired food cost percentage is 30%. Using either the factor method or the product cost percentage method for pricing, what should the price be?
    a. $25.95
    b. $15.30
    c. $19.75
    d. $17.50

5. Use the following information to determine what profit and total revenue equal: price $8.00; number sold 125; expenses $800.
    a. Profit = $3,300, total revenue = $4,500
    b. Profit = $4,231, total revenue = $2,250
    c. Profit = $ 200, total revenue = $1,000
    d. Profit = $1,300, total revenue = $3,365

6. Which of the following is the formula for contribution margin?
    a. Selling price – product cost
    b. Product cost + selling price
    c. Pricing factor/product cost
    d. Selling price x pricing factor

7. What formula is used to determine selling price?
   a. Product cost x contribution margin desired
   b. Pricing factor – product cost
   c. Product cost + contribution margin desired
   d. Desired contribution margin/product cost

8. Out of the following formulas, which one is used to compute pricing factor?
   a. 1.00 x product cost %
   b. 1.00/desired product cost %
   c. Product cost % + 1.00
   d. Desired product cost – 1.00

9. Determine which of the following formulas is used to compute selling price of an item.
   a. Selling price of a specific food item sold x food sales
   b. Cost of food sold/food sales of an item
   c. Food cost % of an item x selling price of a specific food item sold
   d. Cost of a specific food item sold/food cost % of that item

10. Which of the following formulas is used for computing the menu price?
    a. Pricing factor x product cost
    b. Product cost/pricing factor
    c. Selling price x product cost
    d. Selling price/produce cost

11. Use the following information to calculate food cost % of an item: selling price of an item $13.95; cost of a food item sold $5.50. (Round numbers to the nearest whole percent.)
    a. 39%
    b. 45%
    c. 21%
    d. 17%

12. The EP cost of your steak dinner item is $7.75 and your desired food cost percentage is 40%. Using either the factor method or the product cost percentage method for pricing, what should the price be?
    a. $22.75
    b. $19.38
    c. $15.75
    d. $12.50

Chapter Answers to Key Terms & Concepts Review, Discussion Questions, and Quiz Yourself

Key Terms & Concepts Review

1. m	6. f	11. e
2. h	7. l	12. k
3. d	8. c	13. b
4. j	9. n	14. g
5. a	10. i	

Discussion Questions

1. Identify and explain the three major menu formats.
   - Standard menu – This menu is printed, recited by service staff, or otherwise communicated to the guest. The menu is fixed day after day.
   - Daily menu – This menu changes every day. This concept is popular in upscale restaurants.
   - Cycle menu – This menu is in effect for a specific time period. The length of the cycle refers to the length of time the menu is in effect. Typically, cycle menus are repeated on a regular basis.

2. List the nine factors that influence menu price.
   - Local competition
   - Service levels
   - Guest type
   - Product quality
   - Portion size
   - Ambiance
   - Meal period
   - Location
   - Sales mix

3. List and explain two methods of assigning menu prices.
   - Product cost percentage – Product cost should be a predetermined percentage of a selling price. When management uses a predetermined food cost percentage to price menu items, it is stating its belief that product cost in relationship to selling price is of vital importance.
   - Product contribution margin – The amount that remains after the product cost of the menu item is subtracted from the item's selling price. The contribution margin is the amount that "contributes" to paying for labor and other expenses and providing a profit.

4. Identify and explain four of the six special pricing situations.
   - Coupons - Coupons are a popular way to vary menu price. There are two types of coupons in use in the hospitality industry. The first type generally allows the guest to get a free item when he or she buys another item. With the second type, some form of restriction is placed on the coupon's use.
   - Value Pricing – Refers to the practice of reducing all or most prices on the menu in the belief that total guest counts will increase to the point that total sales revenue also increases.
   - Bundling – Refers to the practice of selecting specific menu items and pricing them as a group, in such a manner that the single menu price of the group is lower than if the items comprising the group were purchased individually.
   - Salad bars and buffets – The difficulty in establishing a set price for either a salad bar or a buffet is that total portion cost can vary greatly from one guest to the next. A person weighing 100 pounds will eat a lot less than a person weighing 300 pounds. The secret to keeping the selling price low in a salad bar or buffet is to apply the ABC inventory approach. That is, A items should comprise no more than 20% of the total product available; B items, no more than 30%; and C items, 50%.
   - Bottled wine – Few areas of menu pricing create more controversy than that of pricing wines by the bottle. The reason may be the incredible variance in cost among different vintages, or years of production. How you decide to price the bottled wine offerings on your menu will definitely affect your guest's perception of the price/value relationship offered by your operation.
   - Beverages at receptions and parties – Pricing beverages for open-bar receptions and special events can be very difficult. One way to take care of this problem is to charge the guest for all the drinks he or she actually consumed. Also, maintaining past events and records of what the average consumption for each group of guests has been previously can help you establish an appropriate price.

5. List the four ratings of LEED certification, including levels and points.
   - Certified: 26–32 points
   - Silver: 33–38 points
   - Gold: 39–51 points
   - Platinum: 52–69 points

Quiz Yourself

1. c	7. c
2. b	8. b
3. a	9. d
4. d	10. a
5. c	11. a
6. a	12. b

Chapter 7

Managing the Cost of Labor

Learning Outcomes

At the conclusion of this chapter, you will be able to:

- Identify the factors that affect employee productivity.

- Develop labor standards and employee schedules used in a foodservice operation.

- Analyze and evaluate actual labor utilization.

Study Notes

1. Labor Expense in the Hospitality Industry

- In today's market, labor is so expensive, a manager cannot over staff to meet demand. Other methods must be used to accomplish necessary tasks and stay within the allotted labor budget.

- In some foodservice establishments, the cost of labor actually exceeds the cost of food and beverage products.

- Today's shrinking workforce indicates that managers will find it more difficult to recruit, train, and retain an effective group of employees.

- **Labor Expense** includes salaries and wages, but it consists of other labor-related costs as well.

- Other items included under labor expense vary from operation to operation, but may include such items as: FICA taxes, FUTA (Federal unemployment taxes) and state unemployment taxes, worker's compensation, group life insurance, health insurance, pension plan payments, employee meals, employee training, employee transportation, employee uniforms, employee housing, vacation/sick leave, tuition reimbursement programs, and employee incentives and bonuses.

- **Payroll** refers to the gross pay received by an employee in exchange for his or her work.

- A **salaried employee** receives the same income per week or month regardless of the number of hours worked.

- Salaried employees are actually more accurately described as an **exempt employee** because their duties, responsibilities, and level of decisions make them "exempt" from the overtime provisions of the federal government's Fair Labor Standards Act (FLSA).

- **Minimum staff** is used to designate the least number of employees, or payroll dollars, needed to operate a facility or department within the facility.

- **Fixed Payroll** refers to the amount an operation pays in salaries.

- **Variable Payroll** consists of those dollars paid to hourly employees.

- Variable payroll is added only when management feels it is necessary to provide extra employees in anticipation of an increase in the number of guests to be served.

- Management has little control over fixed labor expense, but nearly 100% control over variable labor expense.

- Labor expense refers to the total of all costs associated with maintaining a foodservice workforce.

- Total labor expense will always exceed that of payroll.

- Payroll is considered a "controllable" labor expense, unlike FICA taxes and insurance premiums. But, in reality, managers may even be able to influence some of the no controllable labor expenses, such as providing a training program to reduce injuries and insurance premiums.

2. Assessing Labor Productivity

- Productivity is the amount of work performed by an employee in a fixed period of time.

- There are many ways to assess labor productivity. In general, productivity is measured in terms of the **productivity ratio** as follows:

$$\frac{\text{Output}}{\text{Input}} = \text{Productivity Ratio}$$

- There are several ways of defining foodservice output and input; thus, there are several types of productivity ratios.

- Foodservice operators must develop their own methods for managing payroll because every food service unit is different.

3. Maintaining a Productive Workforce

- The following are ten key employee-related factors that affect employee productivity:

10 Key Factors Affecting Employee Productivity
1. Employee Selection
2. Training
3. Supervision
4. Scheduling
5. Breaks
6. Morale
7. Menu
8. Convenience vs. Scratch Preparation
9. Equipment/Tools
10. Service Level Desired

- Choosing the right employee is vital in developing a highly productive workforce. The process begins with the development of the job description and job specification.

- A **job description** is a listing of the tasks that must be accomplished by the employee hired to fill a particular position.

- A **job specification** is a listing of the personal characteristics needed to perform the tasks contained in a particular job description.

- When actually beginning to select employees for vacancies, one or more of the following selection aids are normally used: applications, interviews, pre-employment testing, and background/reference checks.

- The employment application is a document completed by the candidate for employment.

- Job interviews, if improperly performed, can subject an employer to significant legal liability.

113

- Pre-employment testing is a common way to help improve employee productivity.

- **Skills tests** can include activities such as typing tests, and computer application tests. **Psychological testing** can include personality tests, tests designed to predict performance, or tests of mental ability. **Pre-employment drug testing** is used to determine if an applicant uses drugs.

- Increasingly, hospitality employers are utilizing background checks prior to hiring employees in selected positions.

- Not conducting background checks on some positions can subject the employer to potential litigation under the doctrine of **negligent hiring**, that is, a failure on the part of an employer to exercise reasonable care in the selection of employees.

- No area under management control holds greater promise for increased employee productivity than job improvement through training.

- Effective training will improve job satisfaction and instill in employees a sense of well-being and accomplishment. It will also reduce confusion, product waste, and loss of guests.

- Effective training begins with a good **orientation program**.

- **Task training** is the training undertaken to ensure an employee has the skills to meet productivity goals.

- The first step in developing a training program is determining how the task is to be done. Once a method for completing a task is developed, it should be strictly enforced unless a better way is developed. Discipline should be administered positively.

- The second step in developing a training program is planning the training session. Taking time to plan the session lets employees know that management is taking it seriously.

- The third step is presenting the training session. Present sessions with enthusiasm. Always make sure that training is presented not because employees "don't know" but rather because management wants them to "know more."

- The fourth step is evaluating the session's effectiveness. Evaluation can be as simple as observing employee behavior or as detailed as preparing written questions, but it must be done to ensure the employees learned.

- The fifth step is retraining at the proper intervals. Employees must be retrained and reminded constantly if their productivity or their skill levels are to remain high.

- All employees require proper supervision.

- Proper supervision means assisting employees in improving productivity.

- When supervision is geared toward helping, the guest benefits and, thus, the operation benefits. This is why it is so important for managers to be **on the floor**, in other words, in the dining area, during meal periods.

- When employees can please both the guests and the manager at once, productivity rises; if employees feel that they can only satisfy the guest *or* the operation, difficulties will arise.

- Even with highly productive employees, poor employee scheduling by management can result in low productivity ratios.

- Proper scheduling ensures that the correct number of employees is available to do the necessary amount of work.

- Scheduling efficiency can often be improved through the use of the **split-shift**, a technique used to match individual employee work shifts with peaks and valleys of customer demand.

- Employees have both a physical and a mental need for breaks from their work.

- Employees need to know that management cares enough to establish a break schedule and stick to it.

- Management should view breaks as a necessary part of maintaining a highly productive workforce, not as lost or wasted time.

- Management must create a fun, motivating environment for employees to work in.

- Motivated groups usually work for a management team that has created a vision, communicated the vision to employees, and ensured that employees share the vision.

- Creating a vision is nothing more than finding a "purpose" for the workforce.

- A shared purpose between management and employees is important for the development and maintenance of high morale.

- Employee turnover *is* high in some sections of the hospitality industry. By some estimates, it exceeds 200% per year. You can measure your turnover by using the following formula:

$$\text{Employee Turnover Rate} = \frac{\text{Number of Employees Separated}}{\text{Number of Employees in Workforce}}$$

- **Separated** is the term used to describe employees who have either quit, been terminated, or in some other manner have "separated" themselves from the operation.

- Some foodservice operators prefer to distinguish between voluntary and involuntary separation.

- A **voluntary separation** is one in which the employee made the decision to leave the organization.

- An **involuntary separation** is one in which management has caused the employee to separate from the organization.

- The turnover formula can be modified to create these two ratios:

$$\text{Involuntary Employee Turnover Rate} = \frac{\text{Number of Employees Involuntarily Separated}}{\text{Number of Employees in Workforce}}$$

$$\text{Voluntary Employee Turnover Rate} = \frac{\text{Number of Employees Voluntarily Separated}}{\text{Number of Employees in Workforce}}$$

- Turnover is expensive. This expense is comprised of actual and hidden costs. Actual costs include interviewing and training time, while hidden costs refer to the number of dishes broken by a new dishwasher, etc.

- A major factor in employee productivity is the foodservice operation's actual menu.

- In general, the more variety of items a kitchen is asked to produce, the less efficient that kitchen will be.

- Menu items must also be selected to complement the skill level of the employees and the equipment available to produce the menu item.

- Since most foodservice operations change their menus infrequently, it is critical that the menu items selected can be prepared efficiently and well.

- The decision of whether to "make" or "buy" involves two major factors, the product quality and the product cost.

- It is important to remember that make or buy decisions affect both food and labor costs.

- Management, often in consultation with kitchen production staff, must resolve make or buy decisions.

- Generally, foodservice productivity ratios have not increased as have those of other businesses, since foodservice is a labor-intensive, rather than machine-intensive industry.

- But, it is critical for the foodservice manager to understand the importance of a properly equipped workplace to improve productivity.

- Equipment should be properly maintained and updated if employees are to be held accountable for productivity standards or gains.

- Today's guest expects and demands higher levels of service than ever before, which requires management to become creative in order to still improve employee productivity.

- When management varies service levels, it varies employee productivity ratios.

- The key to knowing "how many employees are needed" to effectively operate the foodservice unit lies in developing productivity standards.

- The best productivity measure for any unit is, of course, the one that makes the most sense for that unique operation.

4. Measuring Current Labor Productivity

- There are a variety of ways to measure productivity in the hospitality industry such as: labor cost percentage, sales per labor hour, labor dollars per guest served, guests served per labor dollar, guests served per labor hour, revenue available seat hour (RevPASH).

- A very commonly used measure of employee productivity in the foodservice industry is the labor cost percentage.

117

- The labor cost percentage is computed as follows:

$$\frac{\text{Cost of Labor}}{\text{Total Sales}} = \text{Labor Cost \%}$$

- It is important to realize that there are several ways to define cost of labor.

- Controlling the labor cost percentage is extremely important in the foodservice industry since it is the most widely used measure of productivity and thus is often used to determine the effectiveness of a manager.

- Labor cost percentage varies with changes in the price paid for labor. Because of this, labor cost percentage by itself is not a complete measure of workforce productivity.

- The most perishable commodity any foodservice operator buys is the labor hour. When not productively used, it disappears forever.

- This is why many foodservice operators prefer to measure labor productivity in terms of the amount of sales generated for each labor hour used.

$$\frac{\text{Total Sales}}{\text{Labor Hours Used}} = \text{Sales per Labor Hour}$$

- Sales per labor hour will vary with changes in menu selling price, not with changes in the price paid for labor.

- However, sales per labor hour neglects to consider the amount paid to employees per hour to generate the sales.

$$\frac{\text{Cost of Labor}}{\text{Guests Served}} = \text{Labor Dollars per Guest Served}$$

- With labor dollars per guest served, the cost of labor represents all the labor required to serve the guest.

- Labor dollars per guest served varies based on the price paid for labor.

$$\frac{\text{Guests Served}}{\text{Cost of Labor}} = \text{Guests Served per Labor Dollar}$$

118

- As a measure of productivity, guests served per labor dollar expended has advantages. It is relatively easy to compute, and can be used by foodservice units, such as institutions, that do not routinely record dollar sales figures.

$$\frac{\text{Guests Served}}{\text{Labor Hours Used}} = \text{Guests Served per Labor Hour}$$

- Guests served per labor hour is a powerful measure of productivity, not a measure of either cost and productivity or sales and productivity.

- It is extremely useful in comparing similar units in areas with widely differing wage rates or selling prices.

- The managers who use this figure do so because they like the focus of emphasizing service levels and not just reducing costs.

- **Revenue Per Available Seat Hour (RevPASH)** helps managers evaluate how much guests buy and how quickly they are served. It does so primarily by assessing the duration of guests' dining experiences. Duration is simply the length of time customers sit at a table.

$$\frac{\text{Revenue}}{\text{Available Seat Hours}} = \text{Revenue Per Available Seat Hour (RevPASH)}$$

- Many operators prefer to compute their productivity measures on a daily, rather than on a weekly or monthly basis. This can easily be done by using a six-column form with cost of labor, sales, and labor cost %.

- Many operators find that a single measure of their labor productivity is insufficient for their needs.

- Therefore, an operator may establish labor subcategories such as production, service, sanitation, and management.

- When determining labor productivity measures by subcategory remember the following: be sure to include all the relevant data, use the same method to identify the numerator and denominator for each category, compute an overall total to ensure that the sum of the categories is consistent with the overall total.

- Labor costs for each subcategory can be estimated. By following the rules of algebra and adding the word "estimated," the guests served per labor dollar formula can be restated as follows:

$$\frac{\text{Number of Estimated Guests Served}}{\text{Guests Served Per Labor Dollar}} = \text{Estimated Cost of Labor}$$

5. Managing Payroll Costs

- Essentially, the management of payroll costs is a four-step process, which includes the following factors:

    1. Determine productivity standards.
    2. Forecast sales volume.
    3. Schedule employees using productivity standards and forecasted sales volume.
    4. Analyze results.

- A **productivity standard** is defined as management's view of what constitutes an appropriate productivity ratio in a specific foodservice operation.

- Productivity standards represent what you should reasonably expect in the way of output per unit of labor input.

- Productivity standards are typically based on the following types of information: unit history, company average, industry average, management experience, or a combination of some or all of the above.

- A **franchisor** is the entity responsible for selling and maintaining control over the franchise brand's name.

- Sales volume forecasting, when combined with established labor productivity standards, allows a foodservice operator to determine the number of employees needed to effectively service your guests.

- You can establish a labor budget using your productivity standards, your sales forecast, and the labor cost percentage formula you have already learned. Remember that the labor cost percentage formula is defined as:

$$\frac{\text{Cost of Labor}}{\text{Total Sales}} = \text{Labor Cost \%}$$

- If you include the words "forecasted", "standard", and "budget", and follow the rules of algebra, the labor cost percentage formula can be restated as follows:

> **Forecasted Total Sales x Labor Cost % Standard**
> **= Cost of Labor Budget**

- You can establish a budget for total number of labor hours needed to service your establishment. Remember, that guests served per labor hour formula is defined as:

> $$\frac{\text{Guests Served}}{\text{Labor Hours Used}} = \text{Guests Served per Labor Hour}$$

- If you include the words "forecasted," "standard," and "budget," and follow the rules of algebra, the guests served per labor hour formula can be restated as follows:

> $$\frac{\text{Forecasted Number of Guests Served}}{\text{Guests Served per Labor Hour Standard}} = \text{Labor Hours Budget}$$

- Because employee schedules are based upon the number of hours to be worked or dollars to be spent, an employee schedule recap form can be an effective tool in a daily analysis of labor productivity.

- Since labor is purchased on a daily basis, labor costs should be monitored on a daily basis.

- Some foodservice managers practice an **on-call** system whereby employees who are off duty are assigned to on-call status.

- Other managers practice a **call-in** system. In this arrangement, employees who are off duty are required to check in with management on a daily basis to see if the predicted sales volume is such that they may be needed.

- Schedule modifications should be done hourly, if necessary.

- It is critical to match labor usage with projected volume.

- To complete the job of managing labor-related expense, you should analyze your results by comparing actual labor cost to budgeted labor cost. To determine the percentage of budget, the following formula is used:

> $$\frac{\text{Actual Amount}}{\text{Budgeted Amount}} = \text{\% of Budget}$$

- When referring to labor costs, some foodservice operators use the term **standard cost,** which is the labor cost needed to meet established productivity standards, rather than "budgeted cost."

- In the case of labor, we may still be within reasonable budget, though we may vary greatly from the standard. For this reason, the authors prefer the term **budgeted labor** rather than **standard labor**. Labor standards will always vary a bit unless guest counts can be predicted perfectly which, of course, is rarely the case.

6. Reducing Labor-Related Costs

- If management finds that labor costs are too high, problem areas must be identified and corrective action must be taken.

- Ways to reduce fixed labor costs include; improve productivity, increase sales volume, combine jobs to eliminate fixed positions, and reduce wages paid to the fixed payroll employees.

- Ways to reduce variable labor costs include; improve productivity, schedule appropriately to adjust to changes in sales volume, combine jobs to eliminate variable positions, and reduce wages paid to the variable employees.

- One way to increase productivity and reduce labor-related expense is through **employee empowerment**, involving employees in the decision-making process.

- Today, employees have come to realize there is more to life than work. Management, unable to always offer more money, has been forced to come up with new incentives.

- Employees are seeking job satisfaction in addition to salaries or wages.

- Consumers are increasingly aware that when they support businesses committed to sustainability, their dollars impact social and environmental concerns. So committed are they that they are, on average, willing to spend 20% more than the typical guest for products that meet their values and lifestyle.
- In a similar manner, environmentally conscious workers are increasingly becoming aware that a company's care for the environment most often is also reflected in care for its employees. As a result, those companies espousing genuine commitment to the environment attract a more committed and, as a result, a higher quality staff.

7. Technology Tools

- As labor costs continue to increase, and as labor cost management becomes increasingly important to the profitability of restaurateurs, the tools available to manage these costs have increased significantly also.

- Current software programs can help you manage and control labor costs including the following tasks:

  1. Maintain employment records such as:
     a. Required employment documents (i.e., applications, I-9s, W-2s, etc.)
     b. Tax data
     c. Pay rates
     d. Earned vacation or other leave time
     e. Department/cost center affiliation
     f. Benefits eligibility
     g. Training records
  2. Conduct and record the results of on-line or computer-based training programs.
  3. Compute voluntary and involuntary employee turnover rates by department.
  4. Track employee lost days due to injury/accident.
  5. Maintain employee availability records (requested days off, vacation, etc.).
  6. Develop employee schedules and interface employee schedules with time clock systems.
  7. Monitor overtime costs.
  8. Maintain job descriptions and specifications.
  9. Develop and maintain daily, weekly, and monthly productivity reports, including:
     a. Labor cost percentage
     b. Sales per labor hour
     c. Labor dollars per guest served
  10. Interface an employee scheduling component with forecasted sales volume software in the POS system.

Key Terms & Concepts Review

Match the key terms with their correct definitions.

1. Labor expense _____ a. Those dollars spent on employees such as managers, receiving clerks, and dietitians whose presence is not generally directly dependent on the number of guests served.

2. Payroll _____ b. Failure on the part of an employer to exercise reasonable care in the selection of employees.

3. Salaried employee _____ c. The term used to describe employees who have either quit, been terminated, or in some other manner have left their place of employment.

4. Exempt employees _____ d. A listing of the tasks to be performed in a particular position.

5. Minimum staff _____ e. The entity responsible for selling and maintaining control over the franchise name.

6. Fixed payroll _____ f. Pre-employment testing that can include personality tests, tests designed to predict performance, or tests of mental ability.

7. Variable payroll _____ g. Management causes the employee to separate from the organization (fires the employee).

8. Productivity _____ h. An employee who receives the same income per week or month regardless of the number of hours worked.

9. Productivity ratio _____ i. In the case of labor, costs may still be within reasonable budget, though they may vary greatly from the standard.

10. Job description _____ j. The training undertaken to ensure an employee has the skills to meet productivity goals.

11. Job specification _____ k. All expenses (costs), including payroll, required to maintain a workforce in a foodservice operation.

12. Skills test _____ l. In the dining area.

13. Psychological testing _____ m. Giving employees the power to make decisions.

14. Preemployment drug testing	_____	n.	The term used to designate the least number of employees, or payroll dollars, required to operate a facility or department within the facility.
15. Negligent hiring	_____	o.	A system whereby selected employees who are off duty can be contacted by management on short notice to cover for other employees who are absent or to come to work if customer demand suddenly increases.
16. Orientation program	_____	p.	The amount of work performed by a worker in a set amount of time.
17. Task training	_____	q.	A preemployment test used to determine if an applicant uses drugs. It is allowable in most states, and can be a very effective tool for reducing insurance rates and potential employee liability issues.
18. OJT	_____	r.	An employee makes the decision to leave the organization.
19. On the floor	_____	s.	Total wages and salaries paid by a foodservice operation to its employees.
20. Split shift	_____	t.	Management's expectation of the productivity ratio of each employee. Also, management's view of what constitutes the appropriate productivity ratio in a given foodservice unit or units.
21. Separated	_____	u.	A method of training in which workers are training while they actually are performing their required tasks.
22. Voluntary separation	_____	v.	Salaried employees whose duties, responsibilities, and level of decisions make them "exempt" from the overtime provisions of the federal government's Fair Labor Standards Act (FLSA). Exempt employees are expected, by most organizations, to work whatever hours are necessary to accomplish the goals of the organization.

23. Involuntary separation	_____	w.	A system whereby employees who are off duty are required to check in with management on a daily basis to see if the volume is such that they may be needed.
24. Revenue Per Available Seat Hour (RevPASH)	_____	x.	A listing of the personal skills and characteristics needed to perform those tasks pertaining to a particular job description.
25. Productivity standard	_____	y.	Those dollars expended on employees whose presence is directly dependent on the number of guests served. These employees include servers, bartenders, and dishwashers, for example. As the number of guests served increases, the number of these individuals required to do the job also increases. As the number of guests served decreases, variable payroll should decrease.
26. Franchisor	_____	z.	The labor cost needed to meet established productivity standards.
27. On-call	_____	aa.	A scheduling technique used to match individual employee work shifts with the peaks and valleys of customer demand.
28. Call-in	_____	bb.	This formula refers to the total unit output divided by the total unit input.
29. Standard cost	_____	cc.	Pre-employment tests such as typing tests for office employees, computer application tests for those involved in using word processing or spreadsheet tools, or food production tasks, as in the case of chefs.
30. Budgeted labor versus standard labor	_____	dd.	A program usually held during the first week of an employee's job that provides information about important items such as dress code, disciplinary system, tip policy, lockers/security, sick leave policy, and retirement programs.
31. Empowerment	_____	ee.	A measure of how much guests buy and how quickly they are served, calculated as dividing revenue by available seat hours.

Discussion Questions

1. List ten key factors affecting employee productivity.

   _____
   _____
   _____
   _____

2. Identify and explain five ways to measure productivity in the hospitality industry.

   _____
   _____
   _____
   _____

3. List four steps to managing payroll costs.

   _____
   _____
   _____
   _____

4. List the steps for reducing labor-related fixed expenses and variable expenses.

   _____
   _____
   _____
   _____

5. List two advantages of a food service operation's commitment to sustainability.

   _____
   _____
   _____
   _____

Quiz Yourself

Choose the letter of the best answer to the questions listed below.

Use the information below to answer Questions 1 through 5.
Use Brian's last month's operating results to calculate the following productivity standards: labor cost percentage, sales per labor hour, labor dollars per guest served, guests served per labor dollar, guests served per labor hour.

Operating Results for Brian's Caribbean Cafe

Sales Week	# of Guests Served	Labor Hours Used
1	12,000	8,100
2	11,280	7,200
3	10,320	6,400
4	13,200	10,600
Total	46,800	32,300

Average Guest Check	$18
Average Wage per Hour	$7
Total Sales	$842,400
Total Labor Cost	$226,100

Productivity Measurement	Productivity Standard
Labor Cost Percentage	
Sales per Labor Hour	
Labor Dollars per Guest Served	
Guests Served per Labor Dollar	
Guests Served per Labor Hour	

1. Brian's labor cost percentage is:
   a. 32.3%
   b. 26.8%
   c. 24.1%
   d. 29.5%

2. Brian's sales per labor hour is:
   a. $26.08
   b. $23.24
   c. $21.34
   d. $28.55

128

3. Brian's labor dollars per guest served is:
   a. $5.53
   b. $6.75
   c. $4.61
   d. $4.83

4. Brian's guests served per labor dollar is:
   a. 0.18
   b. 0.15
   c. 0.21
   d. 0.24

5. Brian's guests served per labor hour is:
   a. 0.95
   b. 1.45
   c. 2.50
   d. 1.25

6. Which of the following is the employee turnover rate formula?
   a. Number of employees in workforce x number of employees separated
   b. Number of employees in workforce/number of employees separated
   c. Number of employees in workforce + number of employees separated
   d. Number of employees separated/number of employees in workforce

7. Which of the following is the formula for computing sales per labor hour?
   a. Total sales + labor hours used
   b. Total sales/labor hours used
   c. Labor hours used/total sales
   d. Total sales x labor hours used

8. What is the formula for computing the estimated cost of labor?
   a. Number of estimated guests served/guests served per labor dollar
   b. Number of employees x number of estimated guests served
   c. Cost of labor + number of estimated guests served
   d. Guests served per labor dollar/number of estimated guests served

9. Which of the following formulas is used for computing labor hours budget?
   a. Number of guest served x number of labor hours
   b. Forecasted number of guests served + number of labor hours
   c. Forecasted number of guests served/guests served per labor hour standard
   d. Guests served per labor hour standard/forecasted number of guests served

10. What is the formula for computing labor dollars per guest served?
    a. Guests served/cost of labor
    b. Guests served/labor hours used
    c. Forecasted number of guests served/cost of labor
    d. Cost of labor/guests served

11. Calculate the employee turnover rate using the following information: number of employees separated 45; number of employees in workforce 75.
    a. 60%
    b. 1.6%
    c. 56%
    d. 160%

12. Calculate labor cost % using the following information: cost of labor $45,500; total sales $97,000.
    a. 59%
    b. 47%
    c. 35%
    d. 25%

Chapter Answers to Key Terms & Concepts Review, Discussion Questions, and Quiz Yourself

Key Terms & Concepts Review

1. k	6. a	11. x	16. dd	21. c	26. e	31. m
2. s	7. y	12. cc	17. j	22. r	27. o	
3. h	8. p	13. f	18. u	23. g	28. w	
4. v	9. bb	14. q	19. l	24. ee	29. z	
5. n	10. d	15. b	20. aa	25. t	30. i	

Discussion Questions

1. List ten key factors affecting employee productivity.
   - Employee selection
   - Training
   - Supervision
   - Scheduling
   - Breaks
   - Morale
   - Menu
   - Convenience versus scratch preparation
   - Equipment
   - Service level desired

2. Identify and explain five ways to measure productivity in the hospitality industry.
   - Labor cost percentage – Cost of labor includes payroll and total labor costs. Formula for labor cost percentage = cost of labor/total sales
   - Sales per labor hour – The most perishable commodity any foodservice operator buys is the labor hour. When it is not productively used it disappears forever. Formula for sales per labor hour = total sales/labor hours used
   - Labor dollars per guest served – It varies based on the price paid for labor. Formula for labor dollars per gust served = cost of labor/guests served
   - Guests served per labor dollar – It represents all the labor required to serve the guests. Formula for guests served per labor dollar = guests served/cost of labor
   - Guest served per labor hour – Guests served per labor hour is a true measure of productivity, not a measure of either cost and productivity or sales and productivity. It is extremely useful in comparing similar units in areas with widely differing wage rates or selling prices. Formula for guests served per labor hour = guests served/labor hours used

3. List four steps to managing payroll costs.
   - Step 1. Determine Productivity Standards
   - Step 2. Forecast sales volume
   - Step 3. Schedule employees using productivity standards and forecasted sales volume
   - Step 4. Analyze results

4. List the steps for reducing labor-related fixed expenses and variable expenses.
   - Fixed
     - Improve productivity
     - Increase sale volume
     - Combine jobs to eliminate fixed positions
     - Reduce wages paid to the fixed-payroll employees
   - Variable
     - Improve productivity
     - Schedule appropriately to adjust to changes in sales volume
     - Combine jobs to eliminate variable positions
     - Reduce wages paid to the variable employees

5. List two advantages of a food service operation's commitment to sustainability.
   - Customers are, on average, willing to spend 20% more than the typical guest for products that meet their values and lifestyle.
   - Environmentally conscious workers are increasingly becoming aware that a company's care for the environment most often is also reflected in care for its employees. As a result, those companies espousing genuine commitment to the environment attract a more committed and, as a result, a higher quality staff.

Quiz Yourself

1. b	7. b
2. a	8. a
3. d	9. c
4. c	10. d
5. b	11. a
6. d	12. b

Chapter 8

Controlling Other Expenses

Learning Outcomes

At the conclusion of this chapter, you will be able to:

- Categorize Other Expenses in terms of being fixed, variable, or mixed.

- Classify individual Other Expenses as either controllable or non-controllable.

- Compute Other Expense costs in terms of both cost per guest and percentage of sales.

Study Notes

1. Managing Other Expenses

- **Other expenses** are those items that are neither food, beverage, nor labor.

- Other expenses can account for a significant amount of the total cost of operating your foodservice unit.

- You must look for ways to control all of your expenses, but sometimes the environment in which you operate will act upon your facility to influence some of your costs in positive or negative ways.

- In the past, serving water to each guest upon arrival in a restaurant was simply **SOP** (standard operating procedure) for many operations. The rising cost of energy has caused many foodservice operations to implement a policy of serving water on request rather than with each order.

- Energy conservation and waste recycling are two examples of attempts to control and reduce other expenses.

- Each foodservice operation will have its own unique list of required other expenses.

- Another expense can constitute almost anything in the foodservice business.

- If cost groupings are used, they should make sense to the operator and should be specific enough to let the operator know what is in the category.

- Operators can use their own categories, or follow those used in the *Uniform System of Accounts for Restaurants* (USAR).

- While there are many ways in which to assess other expenses, two different considerations of these costs are particularly useful for the foodservice manager. They are:

  1. Fixed, variable, or mixed
  2. Controllable or non-controllable

2. Fixed, Variable, and Mixed Other Expenses

- A **fixed expense** is one that remains constant despite increases or decreases in sales volume.

- A **variable expense** is one that generally increases as sales volume increases, and decreases as sales volume decreases.

- A **mixed expense** is one that has properties of both a fixed and a variable expense.

- The following shows how fixed, variable, and mixed expenses are affected as sales volume increases:

Expense	As a Percentage of Sales	Total Dollars
Fixed Expense	Decreases	Remains the Same
Variable Expense	Remains the Same	Increases
Mixed Expense	Decreases	Increases

- If an operator feels that a fixed expense percentage is too high, he or she must either increase sales or negotiate better rates.

- Normal variations in expense percentage that relate *only* to whether an expense is fixed, variable, or mixed should not be of undue concern to management. It is only when a fixed expense is too high or a variable expense is out of control, that management should act. This is called the concept of **management by exception**.

3. Controllable and Non-controllable Other Expenses

- A **non-controllable expense** is one that the foodservice manager can neither increase nor decrease.

- A **controllable expense** is one in which decisions made by the foodservice manager can have the effect of either increasing or reducing the expense.

- Management should focus its attention on controllable rather than non-controllable expenses.

4. Monitoring Other Expenses

- When managing other expenses, two control and monitoring alternatives are available. They are:

    1. Other expense cost %
    2. Other expense cost per guest

$$\frac{\text{Other Expenses}}{\text{Total Sales}} = \text{Other Expense Cost \%}$$

$$\frac{\text{Other Expense}}{\text{Number of Guests Served}} = \text{Other Expense Cost Per Guest}$$

- The other expense cost per guest formula is of value when management believes it can be helpful, or when lack of a sales figure makes the computation of other expense cost percentage impossible.

- Increasingly, foodservice managers are finding that creative "Green" initiatives benefit their operations in many ways, including those that reduce other expenses. "Trayless dining" is just such an example.

- Trayless operations experience a 30-50% reduction in food and beverage waste. Diners take less food (because they only want to carry what they know they will eat). Without trays to wash, water consumption is also decreased. The result is a decrease in other expenses such as water, utilities, and cleaning products.

5. Reducing Other Expenses

- It is useful to break down other expenses into four categories: food and beverage, labor, facility maintenance, and occupancy when developing strategies for reducing overall other expense costs.

- In general, fixed costs related to food and beverage operations can only be reduced when measuring them as a percentage of total sales. This can be done only by increasing the total sales figure.

- Labor related expenses can also be considered partially fixed and partially variable.

- To reduce costs related to labor, it is necessary to eliminate wasteful labor-related expense.

- However, if an operator attempts to reduce other expenses related to labor too much, he or she may find that the best workers prefer to work elsewhere.

- Reducing employee benefits while attempting to retain a well-qualified workforce is simply management at its worst.

- A properly designed and implemented preventative maintenance program can go a long way toward reducing equipment failure and thus decreasing equipment and facility-related costs.

- Proper care of mechanical equipment prolongs its life and reduces operational costs.

- One way to help ensure that costs are as low as possible is to use a competitive bid process before awarding contracts for services you require.

- In the area of maintenance contracts, for areas such as the kitchen or for mechanical equipment, elevators, or grounds, it is recommended that these contracts be bid at least once per year.

- Air-conditioning, plumbing, heating and refrigerated units should be inspected at least yearly, and kitchen equipment should be inspected at least monthly for purposes of preventative maintenance.

- **Occupancy costs** refer to those expenses incurred by the foodservice unit that are related to the occupancy of and payment for the physical facility it occupies.

6. Technology Tools

- Depending upon the specific food service operation, these costs can represent a significant portion of the operations total expense requirements. As a result, controlling these costs is just as important as controlling food and labor-related costs.

- Software and hardware that can be purchased to assist in this area include applications that relate to:

  1. Assessing and monitoring utilities cost
  2. Minimizing energy costs via the use of motion-activated sensors
  3. Managing equipment maintenance records
  4. Tracking marketing costs/benefits
  5. Menu and promotional materials printing hardware and software
  6. Analysis of communications costs (telephone tolls)
  7. Analysis of all other expense costs on a per-guest basis
  8. Analysis of all other expense costs on a "cost per dollar sale" basis
  9. Comparing building/contents insurance costs across alternative insurance providers
  10. Software designed to assist in the preparation of the income statement, balance sheet, and the statement of cash flows
  11. Income tax management
  12. Income tax filing

- At the minimum, most independent operators should computerize their records related to taxes at all levels to ensure accuracy, safekeeping, and timeliness of required filings.

Key Terms & Concepts Review

Match the key terms with their correct definitions.

1. Other expenses _____

   a. An expense that generally increases as sales volume increases and decreases as sales volume decreases.

2. SOP _____

   b. The measure of electrical usage.

3. Fixed expense _____

   c. The expenses of an operation that are neither food, beverage, nor labor.

4. Variable expense _____

   d. If an expense is within an acceptable variation range, there is no need for management to intervene. Management takes corrective action only when operational results are outside the range of acceptability.

5. Mixed expense _____

   e. Expenses related to occupying and paying for the physical facility that houses the foodservice unit.

6. Management by exception _____

   f. An expense in which the decisions made by the foodservice manager can have the effect of either increasing or reducing the expense.

7. Noncontrollable expense _____

   g. An expense that has properties of both a fixed and a variable expense.

8. Controllable expense _____

   h. A retirement plan in which employees are allowed to contribute money before taxes are assessed.

9. kwh _____

   i. Term used for the way something is done in normal business operations.

10. HVAC _____

    j. An expense that the foodservice manager can neither increase nor decrease.

11. 401(k) _____

    k. An expense that remains constant despite increases or decreases in sales volume.

12. Occupancy costs _____

    l. Heating, ventilation, and air-conditioning

138

Discussion Questions

1. Identify three different types of expenses and their behaviors as sales volume increases.

Expense	As a Percentage of Sales	Total Dollars

2. List four ways a manager can reduce other expenses in the hospitality industry.

_____

_____

_____

_____

3. Define and give examples of controllable and noncontrollable other expenses.

_____

_____

_____

_____

4. Identify two formulas for controlling and monitoring other expenses.

_____

_____

_____

_____

5. Identify two advantages of trayless operations.

_____

_____

_____

_____

Quiz Yourself

Choose the letter of the best answer to the questions listed below.

Haley has kept records of the costs and sales volume of the last four bands she has booked at her bar. Use the information below to answer Questions 1 through 5.

Unit Name: Haley's Bar

Date	Band	Band Expense	Lounge Sales	Cost %	# of Guests Served	Cost Per Guest Served
1/1	The Chick-a-Dees	$8,000	$41,000		4,217	
2/1	Bakers Boys	5,500	30,000		3,800	
3/1	The Staples	6,500	33,000		4,000	
4/1	Guitar Heroes	3,000	20,000		2,500	

1. What is the cost % and cost per guest served for the Chick-a-Dees?
    a. Cost % = 12.3%, cost per guest served = $1.96
    b. Cost % = 19.5%, cost per guest served = $1.90
    c. Cost % = 9.2%, cost per guest served = $1.63
    d. Cost % = 26.1%, cost per guest served = $1.45

2. What is the cost per guest served for the Bakers Boys?
    a. $1.83
    b. $2.02
    c. $1.45
    d. $1.63

3. What is the cost % for the Bakers Boys?
    a. 18.3%
    b. 15.0%
    c. 19.7%
    d. 19.5%

4. Out of the four bands, which band should Haley choose based on cost per guest served?
    a. The Chick-a-Dees
    b. Bakers Boys
    c. The Staples
    d. Guitar Heroes

5. Out of the four bands, which band should Haley choose based on cost %?
    a. The Chick-a-Dees
    b. Bakers Boys
    c. The Staples
    d. Guitar Heroes

6. Out of the four bands, which band has the highest cost %?
   a. The Chick-a-Dees
   b. Bakers Boys
   c. The Staples
   d. Guitar Heroes

7. Out of the four bands, which band has the highest cost per guest served?
   a. The Chick-a-Dees
   b. Bakers Boys
   c. The Staples
   d. Guitar Heroes

8. What formula is used to compute other expense cost %?
   a. Total expenses x total sales
   b. Total sales/other expenses
   c. Other expenses/total sales
   d. Total sales - other expenses

9. Which of the following formulas is used to compute rent expense %?
   a. Rent expense/total sales
   b. Total sales - other expenses
   c. Total sales/rent expense
   d. Rent expense - other expenses

10. Determine which of the following formulas is used to compute other expense cost per guest.
    a. Other expense x number of guests served
    b. Other expense/number of guests served
    c. Number of guests served/other expense
    d. Total expense – other expenses

11. Calculate the other expense cost % (advertising) using the following information: advertising expense $4,500; number of guests served 10,000; total sales $95,000.
    a. 4.7%
    b. 47%
    c. 45%
    d. 4.5%

12. Calculate the other expense cost per guest (advertising) using the following information: advertising expense $4,500; number of guests served 10,000; total sales $95,000.
    a. $0.50
    b. $0.45
    c. $0.47
    d. $4.50

Chapter Answers to Key Terms & Concepts Review, Discussion Questions, and Quiz Yourself

Key Terms & Concepts Review

1. c   6. d   11. h
2. i.   7. j   12. e
3. k   8. f
4. a   9. b
5. g   10. l

Discussion Questions

1. Identify three different types of expenses and their behaviors as sales volume increases.

Expense	As a percentage of sales	Total Dollars
Fixed expense	Decreases	Remains the same
Variable expense	Remains the same	Increases
Mixed expense	Decreases	Increases

2. List four ways a manager can reduce other expenses in the hospitality industry.
   - Reducing costs related to food and beverage operations
   - Reducing costs related to labor
   - Reducing costs related to facility maintenance
   - Reducing occupancy costs

3. Define and give examples of controllable and noncontrollable other expenses.
   - Controllable expense – Decisions made by the foodservice manager can have the effect of either increasing or reducing the expense. Examples of controllable expenses are uniforms, rental equipment, etc.
   - Noncontrollable expense – Foodservice manager can neither increase nor decrease the expense. Examples of noncontrollable expenses are depreciation, insurance premiums, etc.

4. Identify two formulas for controlling and monitoring other expenses.
   - Other expense cost %. Formula for other expense cost % = other expenses/total sales
   - Other expense cost per guest. Formula for other expense cost per guest = other expenses/number of guests served

5. Identify two advantages of trayless operations.
    *   Diners take less food because they only want to carry what they know they will eat. In typical cases, trayless operations experience a 30-50% reduction in food and beverage waste.
    *   Without trays to wash, water consumption is also decreased. The result is a decrease in other expenses such as water, utilities, and cleaning products.

Quiz Yourself

1. b
2. c
3. a
4. d = $1.20
5. d = 15%
6. c = 19.7%

7. a = $1.90
8. c
9. a
10. b
11. a
12. b

Chapter 9

Analyzing Results Using the Income Statement

Learning Outcomes

At the conclusion of this chapter, you will be able to:

- Prepare an income (profit and loss) statement.

- Analyze sales and expenses using the P&L statement.

- Evaluate a facility's profitability using the P&L statement.

Study Notes

1. Introduction to Financial Analysis

- Foodservice managers, more often than not, find themselves awash in numbers! This information, in an appropriate form, is necessary not only to effectively operate your business, but also to serve many interest groups that are directly or indirectly involved with the financial operation of your facility.

- Documenting and analyzing sales, expenses, and profits is sometimes called **cost accounting,** but more appropriately is known as **managerial accounting** to reflect the importance managers place on this process.

- It is important for you to be aware of the difference between bookkeeping, the process of simply recording and summarizing financial data, and the actual analysis of that data.

- Bookkeeping is essentially the summarizing and recording of data. Managerial accounting involves the summarizing, recording, and most importantly, the analysis of those data.

- The United States Congress, in 2002, passed the **Sarbanes-Oxley Act (SOX).** Technically known as the Public Company Accounting Reform and Investor Protection Act, the law provides criminal penalties for those found to have committed accounting fraud.

2. Uniform Systems of Accounts

- Financial reports related to the operation of a foodservice facility are of interest to management, stockholders, owners, creditors, governmental agencies, and, often, the general public.

- To ensure that this financial information is presented in a way that is both useful and consistent, **uniform systems of accounts** have been established for many areas of the hospitality industry.

- The National Restaurant Association has developed *the Uniform System of Accounts for Restaurants* (USAR). The USAR seeks to provide a consistent and clear manner in which managers can record sales, expenses, and the overall financial condition.

- The uniform systems of accounts are guidelines, not a mandated methodology.

3. Income Statement (USAR)

- The **income statement** referred to as the profit and loss (P&L) statement, is a summary report that describes the sales achieved, the money spent on expenses and the resulting profit generated by a business in a specific time period.

- A purpose of the **profit and loss statement** is to identify net income, or the profit generated after all appropriate expenses of the business have been paid.

- Each operation's P&L statement will look slightly different.

- **Net income** is the profit generated after all appropriate expenses of the business have been paid.

- **Fiscal year** is the year established for accounting purposes.

- The USAR can best be understood by dividing it into three sections: gross profit, operating expenses, and nonoperating expenses.

- These three sections are arranged on the income statement *from most controllable to least controllable* by the foodservice manager.

- The **gross profit section** consists of food and beverage sales and those food and beverage related costs that can and should be controlled by the manager on a daily basis.

- The **operating expenses section** is also under the control of the manager but more so on a weekly or monthly basis (with the exception of wages which you can control daily).

- **Nonoperating expenses section** is the least controllable by the foodservice manager. For example, interest paid to creditors as part of short-term or long-term debt repayment is due regardless of the ability of the manager to control day-to-day operating costs.

- The income statement is an **aggregate statement**. This means that all details associated with the sales, cost, and profits of the foodservice establishment are *summarized* on the P&L statement. Although this summary gives the manager a one-shot look at the performance of the operation, the details are not included directly on the statement.

- These details can be found in **supporting schedules**. Each line item on the income statement should be accompanied by a schedule that outlines all of the information that you, as a manager, need to know to operate your business successfully.

- It is in the schedules that you collect the information you need to break down sales or costs and determine problem areas and potential opportunities for improving each item on the income statement.

- Each revenue and expense category on the income statement can be represented both in terms of its whole dollar amount, and its percentage of total sales. All ratios can be calculated as a percentage of *total sales* except the following:

  Food Costs are divided by food sales.

  Beverage Costs are divided by beverage sales.

  Food Gross Profit is divided by food sales.

  Beverage Gross Profit is divided by beverage sales.

- Food and beverage items use their respective food and beverage sales as the denominator so that these items can be evaluated separately from total sales.

- Since food costs and beverage costs are the most controllable items on the income statement, sales and costs need to be separated out of the aggregate and evaluated more carefully.

- The P&L statement is one of several documents that can help evaluate profitability.

4. Analysis of Sales/Volume

- Foodservice operators can measure sales in terms of either dollars or number of guests served. A sales increase or decrease must, however, be analyzed carefully if you are to truly understand the revenue direction of your business.

- Overall sales increases or decreases can be computed using the following steps:

  1. Determine sales for this accounting period.
  2. Calculate the following: this period's sales minus last period's sales.
  3. Divide the difference in #2 above by last period's sales to determine percentage variance.

- There are several ways a foodservice operation experiences total sales volume increases. These are:

  1. Serve the same number of guests at a higher check average.
  2. Serve more guests at the same check average.
  3. Serve more guests at a higher check average.
  4. Serve *fewer* guests at a *much* higher check average.

- The procedure to adjust sales variance to include known menu price increases is as follows:

  Step 1. Increase prior period sales (last year) by amount of the price increase.
  Step 2. Subtract the result in Step 1 from this period's sales.
  Step 3. Divide the difference in Step 2 by the value of Step 1.

- Every critical factor must be considered when evaluating sales revenue including the number of operating meal periods or days; changes in menu prices, guest counts, and check averages; and special events.

5. Analysis of Food Expense

- For the effective foodservice manager, the analysis of food expense is a matter of major concern.

- It is important to remember that the numerator of the food cost % equation is cost of food sold while the denominator is total food sales, rather than total food and beverage sales.

- A food cost percentage can be computed for each food subcategory. For instance, the cost percentage for the category Meats and Seafood would be computed as follows:

> **Meats and Seafood Cost**
> **Total Food Sales** = Meats and Seafood Cost %

- **Inventory turnover** refers to the number of times the total value of inventory has been purchased and replaced in an accounting period.

- The formula used to compute inventory turnover is as follows:

> **Cost of Food Consumed**
> **Average Inventory Value** = Food Inventory Turnover

- Note that it is cost of food consumed rather than cost of food sold that is used as the numerator in this ratio. This is because all food inventories should be tracked so that you can better determine what is sold, wasted, spoiled, pilfered, or provided to employees as employee meals.

- Be sure that a high inventory turnover is caused by increased sales and not by increased food waste, food spoilage, or employee theft.

- The average inventory value is computed by adding beginning inventory for this period to the ending inventory from this period and dividing by 2 as follows:

> **Beginning Inventory Value + Ending Inventory Value**
> **2**
> **= Average Inventory Value**

6. Analysis of Beverage Expense

- Beverage inventory turnover is computed using the following formula:

> **Cost of Beverages Consumed**
> **Average Beverage Inventory Value** = Beverage Inventory Turnover

- If an operation carries a large number of rare and expensive wines, it will find that its beverage inventory turnover rate is relatively low. Conversely, those beverage operations that sell their products primarily by the glass are likely to experience inventory turnover rates that are quite high.

- Similar to the method for adjusting sales, the method for adjusting expense categories for known cost increases is as follows:
  - Step 1. Increase prior-period expense by amount of cost increase.
  - Step 2. Determine appropriate sales data, remembering to adjust prior-period sales, if applicable.
  - Step 3. Divide costs determined in Step 1 above by sales determined in Step 2 above.

148

- All food and beverage expense categories must be adjusted both in terms of costs and selling price if effective comparisons are to be made over time.

- As product costs increase or decrease, and as menu prices change, so too will food and beverage expense percentages change.

7. Analysis of Labor Expense

- When total dollar sales volume increases, fixed labor cost percentages will decline.

- Variable labor costs will increase along with sales volume increases, but the percentage of revenue they consume should stay constant.

- When you combine a declining percentage (fixed labor cost) with a constant one (variable labor cost), you should achieve a reduced overall percentage, although your total labor dollars expended can be higher.

- Declining costs of labor may be the result of significant reductions in the number of guests served.

- Salaries and wages expense percentage is computed as follows:

$$\frac{\text{Salaries and Wages Expense}}{\text{Total Sales}} = \text{Salaries and Wages Expense \%}$$

- Just as adjustments must be made for changes in food and beverage expenses before valid expense comparisons can be made, so too must adjustments be made for changes, if any, in the price an operator pays for labor such as a **COLA** (cost of living adjustment), or raise.

- Adjust both sales and cost of labor using the same steps as those employed for adjusting food or beverage cost percentage and compute a new labor cost as follows:
  - Step 1. Determine sales adjustment.
  - Step 2. Determine total labor cost adjustment.
  - Step 3. Compute adjusted labor cost percentage.

- This year's projected labor cost is computed as follows:

$$\text{This Year's Sales} \times \text{Last Year's Adjusted Labor Cost \%} = \text{This Year's Projected Labor Cost}$$

- Increases in payroll taxes, benefit programs, and employee turnover all can affect labor cost percentage.

- One of the fastest increasing labor-related costs for foodservice managers today is cost of health insurance benefit programs.

8. Analysis of Other Expense

- For comparison purposes, managers are able to use industry trade publications to get national averages on other expense categories. One helpful source is an annual publication, the *Restaurant Industry Operations Report* published by the National Restaurant Association and prepared by Deloitte & Touche (can be ordered through www.restaurant.org).

- For operations that are a part of a corporate chain, unit managers can receive comparison data from district and regional managers who can chart performance against those of other operators in the city, region, state, and nation.

9. Analysis of Profits

- Profit percentage using the profit margin formula is as follows:

$$\frac{\text{Net Income}}{\text{Total Sales}} = \text{Profit Margin}$$

- **Profit margin** is also known as **return on sales**, or **ROS**. For the foodservice manager perhaps no number is more important than ROS. This percentage is the most telling indicator of a manager's overall effectiveness at generating revenues and controlling costs in line with forecasted results.

- While it is not possible to state what a "good" ROS figures should be for all restaurants, industry averages, depending on the specific segment, range from 1% to over 20%.

- Some operators prefer to use operating income (see Figure 9.1) as the numerator for profit margin instead of net income. This is because interest and income taxes are considered non-operating expenses and thus, not truly reflective of a manger's ability to generate a profit.

- Profit variance % for the year can be measured by the following formula:

$$\frac{\text{Net Income This Period} - \text{Net Income Last Period}}{\text{Net Income Last Period}} = \text{Profit Variance \%}$$

- Monitoring selling price, guest counts, sales per guest, operating days, special events, and actual operating costs is necessary for accurate profit comparisons. Without knowledge of each of these areas, the effective analysis of profits becomes a risky proposition.

- Perceptive foodservice operators now clearly recognize that profits, planet, and people all benefit from an operation's green commitment.

- "Planet friendly" management yields many positive financial outcomes for businesses, as well as for the health of the local communities these businesses count on to support them.

- Buying local (to minimize transportation costs and environmental impact) creates relationships with those who produce food and keeps money flowing through a local economy, resulting in a healthier community and reduced health care costs.

10. Technology Tools

- This chapter introduced the concept of management analysis as it relates to sales, expenses, and profits. In this area, software is quite advanced and the choice of tools available to help you with your own analyses is many. The best of the programs on the market will:

    1. Analyze operating trends (sales and costs) over management-established time periods.
    2. Analyze food and beverage costs.
    3. Analyze labor costs.
    4. Analyze other expenses.
    5. Analyze profits.
    6. Compare operating results of multiple profit centers within one location or across several locations.
    7. Interface with an operation's point of sales (POS) system or even incorporate it completely.
    8. Red flag" areas of potential management concern.
    9. Evaluate the financial productivity of individual servers, day parts, or other specific time periods established by management.
    10. Compare actual to budgeted results and compute variance percentages as well as suggest revisions to future budget periods based on current operating results.

Key Terms & Concepts Review

Match the key terms with their correct definitions.

1. Cost accounting /   _____   a. The profit realized after all
   Managerial accounting   expenses and appropriate taxes for
                                                a business have been paid.

2. Bookkeeping   _____   b. A report that describes the sales
                                                achieved, the money spent on
                                                expenses and the resulting profit
                                                generated by a business in a
                                                specific time period.

3. Sarbanes-Oxley Act (SOX) _____   c. Summary of all details associated
                                                with the sales, costs, and profits of
                                                a foodservice establishment.

4. Uniform system of   _____   d. This formula refers to net income
   accounts   divided by total revenues.

5. Income statement / Profit _____   e. The process of documenting and
   and loss (P&L) statement   analyzing sales, expenses, and
                                                profits.

6. Net income   _____   f. Covers Sales through Total Gross
                                                Profit on the Uniform System of
                                                Accounts for Restaurants income
                                                statement. Consists of food and
                                                beverage sales and costs that can
                                                and should be controlled by the
                                                manager on a daily basis.

7. Fiscal year   _____   g. List of all details associated with
                                                each line item on the income
                                                statement.

8. Gross profit section (of   _____   h. The process of recording
   the USAR)   and summarizing financial
                                                data.

9. Operating expenses   _____   i. Cost of living adjustment; a term
   section (of the USAR)   used to describe a raise in
                                                employee pay.

10. Nonoperating expenses   _____   j. The number of times the total
    section (of the USAR)   value of inventory has been
                                                purchased and replaced in an
                                                accounting period.

11. Aggregate statement _____ k. Technically known as the Public Company Accounting Reform and Investor Protection Act, the law provides criminal penalties for those found to have committed accounting fraud.

12. Supporting schedules _____ l. Covers Interest through Net Income on the Uniform System of Accounts for Restaurants income statement. It is this section that is least controllable by the foodservice manager.

13. Inventory turnover _____ m. Covers Operating Expenses through Operating Income on the Uniform System of Accounts for Restaurants income statement. Consists of expenses under the control of the manager on a weekly or monthly basis.

14. COLA _____ n. Standardized sets of procedures used for categorizing revenue and expense in a defined industry.

15. Profit margin / Return on Sales (ROS) _____ o. Start and stop dates for a 365-day accounting period. This period need not begin in January and end in December.

Discussion Questions

1. Identify and define the system of accounts that the National Restaurant Association developed.

   _____

   _____

   _____

   _____

2. Explain what the income statement is and the three sections that are part of this statement.

   _____

   _____

   _____

   _____

3. Identify and define the act that was passed by the United Stated Congress in 2002 regarding fraudulently reported financial information.

   _____

   _____

   _____

   _____

4. List the six areas of the income statement that a manager should analyze.

   _____

   _____

   _____

   _____

5. List five advantages of buying local products.

   _____

   _____

   _____

   _____

Quiz Yourself

Choose the letter of the best answer to the questions listed below.

1. Calculate the sales variance in dollars and as a percentage given the following information: last year's sales $10,000,000; this year's sales $12,000,000.
   a. Sales variance = $4,000,000; sales variance percentage = 40%
   b. Sales variance = $2,500,000; sales variance percentage = 25%
   c. Sales variance = $2,000,000; sales variance percentage = 20%
   d. Sales variance = $3,000,000; sales variance percentage = 30%

2. Calculate the beverage inventory turnover given the following information: cost of beverages consumed $150,000; beginning inventory $12,000; ending beverage inventory $19,000; beverage sales $940,000.
   a. 15%
   b. 9.7 times
   c. 29%
   d. 4.5 times

3. Calculate average inventory value given the following information: expenses $12,000; ending inventory $26,000; beginning inventory $50,000.
   a. $38,000
   b. $55,000
   c. $23,000
   d. $95,000

4. Calculate salaries and wages expense % given the following information: total sales $9,000,000; salaries and wages expense $3,700,000; other expense $2,200,000.
   a. 52%
   b. 63%
   c. 24%
   d. 41%

5. Calculate this year's projected labor cost given the information below: last year's adjusted labor cost % 25%; this year's sales $4,250,000.
   a. $2,052,368
   b. $3,156,783
   c. $1,062,500
   d. $2,250,165

6. What is the formula for food inventory turnover?
   a. Cost of food consumed/average inventory value
   b. Average inventory value/cost of food consumed
   c. Food sales/average inventory value
   d. Average inventory value/food sales

7. Which of the following is the formula for average inventory value?
   a. Average inventory/2
   b. Beginning inventory/ending inventory
   c. Beginning inventory + ending inventory/2
   d. Beginning inventory – ending inventory/2

8. Determine which of the following is the formula salaries and wages expense %?
   a. Total sales/salaries and wages expense
   b. Salaries and wages expense/total sales
   c. Salaries and wages expense + total sales
   d. Total sales – salaries and wages expense

9. Identify the formula below for this year's projected labor cost.
   a. This year's sales/last year's labor cost
   b. This year's sales – last year's sales/last year's sales
   c. This year's sales + last year's labor cost
   d. This year's sales x last year's adjusted labor cost %

10. What is the formula for profit margin?
    a. Net income/total sales
    b. Total sales/net income
    c. Net income this period – net income last period/net income this period
    d. Net income this period – net income last period

11. Calculate marketing expense % given the following information: total sales $7,000,000; marketing expense $250,000; total expense $6,160,000.
    a. 3.6%
    b. 4.1%
    c. 17%
    d. 14%

12. Calculate this year's projected labor cost given the information below: last year's adjusted labor cost % 30%; this year's sales $6,150,000.
    a. $3,529,456
    b. $1,845,000
    c. $1,365,500
    d. $2,178,123

Chapter Answers to Key Terms & Concepts Review, Discussion Questions, and Quiz Yourself

Key Terms & Concepts Review

1. e	6. a	11. c
2. h	7. o	12. g
3. k	8. f	13. j
4. n	9. m	14. i
5. b	10. l	15. d

Discussion Questions

1. Identify and define the system of accounts that the National Restaurant Association developed.
   - Uniform System of Accounts for Restaurants (USAR) – Standardized set of procedures used for categorizing revenue and expenses in the restaurant industry.

2. Explain what the income statement is and the three sections that are part of this statement.
   - Income statement – A detailed listing of revenue and expenses for a given accounting period (also referred to as the Profit and Loss Statement).
     - Gross profit section – consists of food and beverage sales and costs that can and should be controlled by a manager.
     - Operating expenses section - under control by the manager but more on a weekly or monthly basis.
     - Non operating expense section – least controllable by the foodservice manager. Covers interest through net income.

3. Identify and define the act that was passed by the United Stated Congress in 2002 regarding fraudulently reported financial information.
   - Sarbanes-Oxley Act (SOX) - Technically known as the Public Company Accounting Reform and Investor Protection Act, the law provides criminal penalties for those found to have committed accounting fraud.

4. List the six areas of the income statement that a manager should analyze.
   - Sales/volume
   - Food expense
   - Beverage expense
   - Labor expense
   - Other expense
   - Profits

5. List five advantages of buying local products.
    *   Positive financial outcomes for businesses
    *   Minimize transportation costs and environmental impact
    *   Community connection
    *   Positive nutrition and health impacts within the community
    *   A reduction in health care costs

Quiz Yourself

1. c	7. c
2. b	8. b
3. a	9. d
4. d	10. a
5. c	11. a
6. a	12. b

Chapter 10

Planning for Profit

Learning Outcomes

At the conclusion of this chapter, you will be able to:

- Analyze a menu for profitability.

- Prepare a cost/volume/profit (break-even) analysis.

- Establish a budget and monitor performance to the budget.

Study Notes

1. Financial Analysis and Profit Planning

- In addition to analyzing the P&L statement, you should also undertake a thorough study of three areas that will assist you in planning for profit. These three areas of analysis are menu analysis, cost/volume/profit (CVP) analysis, and budgeting.

- Whereas menu analysis concerns itself with the profitability of the menu items you sell, CVP analysis deals with the sales dollars and volume required by your foodservice unit to avoid an operating loss and to make a profit. The process of budgeting allows you to plan your next year's operating results by projecting sales, expenses, and profits to develop a budgeted P&L statement.

2. Menu Analysis

- Menu analysis involves marketing, sociology, psychology, and emotions. Remember that guests respond best not to weighty financial analyses, but rather to menu item descriptions, the placement of items on the menu, their price, and their current popularity.

- Many components of the menu such as pricing, layout, design, and copy play an important role in the overall success of a foodservice operation.

- Three of the most popular systems of menu analysis are food cost %, contribution margin, and goal value analysis. (See figure 10.1)
- The **matrix analysis** provides a method for comparisons between menu items.

- A matrix allows menu items to be placed into categories based on whether they are above or below menu item averages for factors such as food cost %, popularity, and contribution margin.

- When analyzing a menu using the food cost percentage method, you are seeking menu items that have the effect of minimizing your overall food cost percentage.

- The characteristics of the menu items that fall into each of the four matrix squares are unique and thus should be marketed differently. (See figure 10.3)

- When analyzing a menu using the contribution margin approach, the operator seeks to produce a menu that maximizes the overall contribution margin.

- **Contribution margin per menu item** is defined as the amount that remains after the product cost of the menu item is subtracted from the item's selling price.

- Contribution margin per menu item would be computed as follows:

> **Selling Price – Product Cost**
> **= Contribution Margin per Menu Item**

- To determine the total contribution margin for the menu, the following formula is used:

> **Total Sales – Total Product Costs = Total Contribution Margin**

- You can determine the average contribution margin per item, using the following formula:

> **Total Contribution Margin**
> **Number of Items Sold**
> **= Average Contribution Margin per Item**

- Contribution margin is the amount that you will have available to pay for your labor and other expenses and to keep for your profit.

- When contribution margin is the driving factor in analyzing a menu, the two variables used for the analysis are contribution margin and item popularity.

- Each of the menu items that fall in the squares requires a special marketing strategy, depending on its square location. (See figure 10.4)

- A frequent and legitimate criticism of the contribution margin approach to menu analysis is that it tends to favor high-priced menu items over low-priced ones, since higher priced menu items, in general, tend to have the highest contribution margins.

- The selection of either food cost percentage or contribution margin as a menu analysis technique is really an attempt by the foodservice operator to answer the following questions:

  1. Are my menu items priced correctly?
  2. Are the individual menu items selling well enough to warrant keeping them on the menu?
  3. Is the overall profit margin on my menu items satisfactory?

- Some users of the contribution margin method of menu analysis refer to it as **menu engineering** and classify the squares used in the analysis with colorful names. The most common of these are "Plow horses" (square 1), "Stars" (square 2), "Dogs" (square 3), and "Puzzles" or sometimes "Challenges" (square 4).

- Goal value analysis uses the power of an algebraic formula to replace less sophisticated menu averaging techniques.

- The advantages of goal value analysis are many, including ease of use, accuracy, and the ability to simultaneously consider more variables than is possible with two-dimensional matrix analysis.

- **Goal value analysis** does evaluate each menu item's food cost percentage, contribution margin, and popularity and, unlike the two previous analysis methods introduced, however, it includes the analysis of the menu item's nonfood variable costs as well as its selling price.

- Menu items that achieve goal values higher than that of the menu's overall goal value will contribute greater than average profit percentages. As the goal value for an item increases, so too, does its profitability percentage.

- The goal value formula is as follows:

$$A \times B \times C \times D = \text{Goal Value}$$

Where

A = 1.00 – Food Cost %
B = Item Popularity
C = Selling Price
D = 1.00 – (Variable Cost % + Food Cost %)

- The computed goal value carries no unit designation; that is, it is neither a percentage nor a dollar figure because it is really a numerical target or score.

- Every menu will have items that are more or less profitable than others.

- A **loss leader** is a menu item that is priced very low, sometimes even below total costs, for the purpose of drawing large numbers of guests to the operation.

- Items that do not achieve the targeted goal value tend to be deficient in one or more of the key areas of food cost percentage, popularity, selling price, or variable cost percentage.

- In theory, all menu items have the potential of reaching the goal value. Management may, however, determine that some menu items can best serve the operation as loss leaders, an approach illustrated by the continued use of "value" menu items by leading chains in the **Quick Service Restaurant (QSR)** segment.

- Goal value analysis will allow you to make better decisions more quickly. Goal value analysis is also powerful because it is not, as is matrix analysis, dependent on past performance to establish profitability but can be used by management to establish future menu targets.

- A purely quantitative approach to menu analysis is neither practical nor desirable. Menu analysis and pricing decisions are always a matter of experience, skill, insight and educated predicting.

3. Cost/Volume/Profit Analysis

- Each foodservice operator knows that some accounting periods are more profitable than others. Often, this is because sales volume is higher or costs are lower during certain periods. Profitability, then, can be viewed as existing on a graph similar to the following:

Cost/Volume/Profit Graph

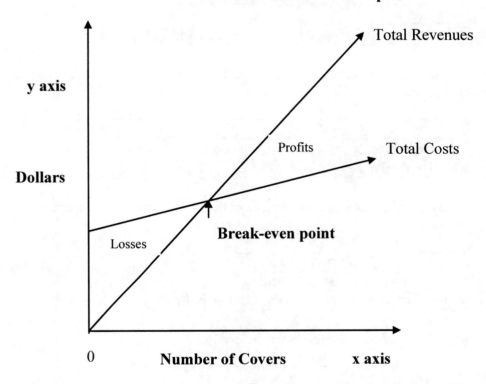

- At the **break-even point**, operational expenses are exactly equal to sales revenue; below the break-even point, costs are higher than revenues, so losses occur; above the break-even point, revenues exceed costs, so profits are made.

- A **cost/volume/profit (CVP) analysis** helps predict the sales dollars and volume required to achieve desired *profit* (or break-even) based on your known costs.

- CVP calculations can be done on either; 1.) the dollar sales volume required to break even or achieve the desired profit, or 2.) the number of guests (covers) required that must be served to break even.

- A **contribution margin income statement** simply shows P&L items in terms of sales, variable costs, contribution margin, fixed costs, and profit. (See figure 10.9)

- **Contribution margin for the overall operation** is defined as the dollar amount that *contributes* to covering fixed costs and providing for a profit.

- Contribution margin is calculated as follows:

Total Sales − Variable Costs = Contribution Margin

- To determine the dollar sales required to break even, use the following formula:

  $$\frac{\text{Fixed Costs}}{\text{Contribution Margin \%}} = \text{Break-Even Point in Sales}$$

- In terms of the number of guests that must be served in order to break even, use the following formula:

  $$\frac{\text{Fixed Costs}}{\text{Contribution Margin per Unit (Guests)}} = \text{Break-Even Point in Guests Served}$$

- To determine sales dollars and covers to achieve the after tax profit goal, use the following formula:

  $$\frac{\text{Fixed Costs + Before-Tax Profit}}{\text{Contribution Margin \%}} = \text{Sales Dollars to Achieve Desired After-Tax Profit}$$

- To convert after-tax profit to before-tax profit, compute the following:

  $$\frac{\text{After Tax Profit}}{\text{1-Tax Rate}} = \text{Before-Tax Profit}$$

- In terms of calculating the number of guests that must be served in order to make the desired after-tax profit, use the following formula:

  $$\frac{\text{Fixed Costs + Before-Tax Profit}}{\text{Contribution Margin per Unit (Guest)}} = \text{Guests to Be Served to Achieve Desired After-Tax Profit}$$

- When calculating sales and covers to achieve break-even and desired after-tax profits, you can easily remember which formulas to use if you know the following:

  1. Contribution Margin % is used to calculate sales *dollars*.
  2. Contribution Margin per *unit* is used to calculate sales volume in *units* (guests).

164

- Once you fully understand the CVP analysis concepts, you can predict any sales level for break-even or after-tax profits based on your selling price, fixed costs, variable costs, and contribution margin.

- Cost/volume/profit analysis is used to establish targets for the entire operation, whereas, goal value analysis evaluates individual menu items against those operational targets. Therefore, the two analyses can be strategically linked.

Cost/Volume/Profit Analysis	Goal Value Analysis
Food cost % from contribution margin income statement	Food cost % goal
Guests served to achieve desired after-tax profit	Total average number of covers per menu item goal
Selling price	Selling price goal
Labor and other variable cost % from contribution margin income statement	Variable cost % goal

- By looking at these two analyses, you can learn how the overall goals of the operation affect menu item profitability. Conversely, you can see how changes you make to menu items affect the overall profitability of the operation.

- **Minimum Sales Point (MSP)** is the sales volume required to justify staying open for a given period of time.

- The information needed to calculate a MSP is:
    1. Food cost %
    2. Minimum payroll cost needed for the time period
    3. Variable cost %

- Fixed costs are eliminated from the calculation because even if volume of sales equals zero, fixed costs still exist and must be paid.

- In calculating MSP, food cost % + variable cost % is called the **minimum operating cost**.

- The MSP formula is shown as follows:

$$\frac{\text{Minimum Labor Cost}}{1 - \text{Minimum Operating Cost}} = \text{MSP}$$

or

$$\frac{\text{Minimum Labor Cost}}{1 - (\text{Food Cost \%} + \text{Variable Cost \%})} = \text{MSP}$$

- Corporate policy, contractual hours, promotion of a new unit, competition, and other factors must all be taken into account before the decision is made to modify operational hours.

4. The Budget

- The **budget**, or financial plan, will detail the operational direction of your unit and your expected financial results.

- The budget should not be a static document. It should be modified and fine-tuned as managerial accounting presents data about sales and costs that affect the direction of the overall operation.

- Just as the P&L tells you about your past performance, the budget is developed to help you achieve your future goals.

$$\boxed{\text{Budgeted Revenue} - \text{Budgeted Expense} = \text{Budgeted Profit}}$$

- To prepare the budget and stay within it assures you predetermined results.

- The effective foodservice operator builds his or her budget, monitors it closely, modifies it when necessary, and achieves the desired results.

- Budgeting is best done by the entire management team, for it is only through participation in the process that the whole organization will feel compelled to support the budget.

- Foodservice budgets can be considered as one of three main types: long-range budget, annual budget, and achievement budget.

- The **long-range budget** is typically prepared for a period of three to five years.

166

- The **annual budget** is for a one-year period or, in some cases, one season. An annual budget need not follow a calendar year. An annual budget need not consist of 12, one-month periods. While many operators prefer one-month budgets, some prefer budgets consisting of 13, 28-day periods, while others use quarterly (three-month) or even weekly budgets to plan for revenues and costs throughout the budget year.

- The **achievement budget** is always of a shorter range, perhaps a month or a week. It provides current operating information and thus assists in making current operational decisions.

5. Developing the Budget

- To establish any type of budget, you need to have the following information available:

    1. Prior-period operating results
    2. Assumptions of next-period operations
    3. Goals
    4. Monitoring policies

- To determine a food budget, compute the estimated food cost as follows:

> 1. **Last Year's Food Cost per Meal = Last Year's Cost of Food / Total Meals Served**
>
> 2. **Last Year's Food Cost per Meal + % Estimated Increase in Food Cost = This Year's Food Cost per Meal**
>
> 3. **This Year's Food Cost Per Meal x Number of Meals to Be Served This Year = Estimated Cost of Food This Year**

- To determine a labor budget, compute the estimated labor cost as follows:

> 1. **Last Year's Labor Cost per Meal = Last Year's Cost of Labor / Total Meals Served**
>
> 2. **Last Year's Labor Cost per Meal + % Estimated Increase in Labor Cost = This Year's Labor Cost per Meal**
>
> 3. **This Year's Labor Cost per Meal x Number of Meals to Be Served This Year = Estimated Cost of Labor This Year**

- Budgeting for utility costs is one a foodservice operator's biggest challenges. This is due to both the instability of energy prices and the impact of the weather on usage.

- Strategies for reducing energy usage should include:

    1. Investigating the instillation of smart lighting systems that automatically turn off lights when storage areas are vacant.
    2. Replacement of all incandescent lighting with an appropriate type of electric discharge lamp (such as fluorescent, mercury vapor, metal halide or sodium) wherever possible.
    3. The use of dual-flush, low-flow or waterless toilets to reduce water waste.
    4. Installing low-flow faucet aerators on all sinks to cut water usage by as much as 40%; from a standard 4 gallons per minute to a cost-saving 2.5 gallons a minute.
    5. Implementation of an effective preventive maintenance program for all cooking equipment including frequent and accurate temperature recalibrations.
    6. Reducing waste disposal costs by implementing effective source reduction plans as well as pre and post-production recycling efforts.

6. Monitoring the Budget

- In general, the budget should be monitored in each of the following three areas:

    1. Revenue
    2. Expense
    3. Profit

- Some foodservice operators relate revenue to the number of seats they have available in their operation. The formula for the computation of sales per seat is as follows:

$$\frac{\text{Total Sales}}{\text{Available Seats}} = \text{Sales per Seat}$$

- Some commercial foodservice operators relate revenue to the number of square feet their operations occupy. These operators budget revenues based on a **sales per square foot** basis. The formula of sales per square foot is as follows:

$$\frac{\text{Total Sales}}{\text{Total Square Footage Occupied}} = \text{Sales per Square Foot}$$

- Effective managers compare their actual revenue to that which they have projected on a regular basis.

- If revenue should fall below projected levels, the impact on profit can be substantial.

- Effective foodservice managers are careful to monitor operational expense because costs that are too high or too low may be cause for concern.

- Some operators elect to utilize the **yardstick method** of calculating expense standards so determinations can be made as to whether variations in expenses are due to changes in sales volume, or other reasons such as waste or theft.

- Developing Yardstick Standards for Food

  Step 1. Divide total inventory into management-designated sub-groups, for example, meats, produce, dairy, and groceries.
  Step 2. Establish dollar value of subgroup purchases for prior accounting period.
  Step 3. Establish sales volume for the prior accounting period.
  Step 4. Determine percentage of purchasing dollar spent for each food category.
  Step 5. Determine percentage of revenue dollar spent for each food category.
  Step 6. Develop weekly sales volume and associated expense projection. Compute % cost to sales for each food grouping and sales estimate.
  Step 7. Compare weekly revenue and expense to projection. Correct if necessary.

- Developing Yardstick Standards for Labor

  Step 1. Divide total labor cost into management-designated sub-groups, for example, cooks, warewashers, and bartenders.
  Step 2. Establish dollar value spent for each subgroup during the prior accounting period.
  Step 3. Establish sales volume for the prior accounting period.
  Step 4. Determine percentage of labor dollar spent for each subgroup.
  Step 5. Determine percentage of revenue dollar spent for each labor category.
  Step 6. Develop weekly sales volume and associated expense projection. Compute % cost to sales for each labor category and sales estimate.
  Step 7. Compare weekly revenue and expense to projection. Correct if necessary.

- As business conditions change, changes in the budget are to be expected. This is because budgets are based on a specific set of assumptions, and if these assumptions change, so too will the budgets.

- Budgeted profit levels must be realized if an operation is to provide adequate returns for owner and investor risk.

- The primary purpose of management is to generate the profits needed to continue the business. Budgeting for these profits is a fundamental step in the process.

7. Technology Tools

- While menu analysis software is often packaged as part of a larger program and is somewhat limited, the software required to do an overall break-even analysis is readily available, as well as that required for budgeting. Specialized software in this area is available to help you:

  1. Evaluate item profitability.
  2. Conduct menu matrix analysis.
  3. Perform break-even analysis.
  4. Budget revenue and expense levels.
  5. Budget profit levels.
  6. Assemble budgets based on days, weeks, months, years, or other identifiable accounting periods.
  7. Conduct performance to budget analysis.
  8. Maintain performance to budget histories.
  9. Blend budgets from multiple profit centers (or multiple units).
  10. Perform budgeted cash flow analysis.

- For commercial operators, it is simply not wise to attempt to operate an effective foodservice unit without a properly priced menu and an accurate budget that reflects estimated sales and expense levels.

Key Terms & Concepts Review

Match the key terms with their correct definitions.

1. Matrix analysis _____   a. A forecast or estimate of projected revenue, expense, and profit for a period of one year.

2. Contribution margin per menu item _____   b. A financial summary that shows P&L items in terms of sales, variable costs, contribution margin, fixed costs, and profit.

3. Menu engineering _____   c. A forecast or estimate of projected revenue, expense, and profit for a period of three to five years.

4. Goal value analysis _____   d. Method of calculating expense standards so determinations can be made as to whether variations in expenses are due to changes in sales volume or other reasons such as waste or theft.

5. Loss leader _____   e. A method for comparisons between menu items. A matrix allows menu items to be placed into categories based on whether they are above or below overall menu item averages such as food cost %, popularity, and contribution margin.

6. Quick service restaurant (QSR) _____   f. The dollar amount that contributes to covering fixed costs and providing for a profit.

7. Break-even point _____   g. A forecast or estimate of projected revenue, expense, and profit for a period of a month or a week. It provides current operating information and, thus, assists in making current operational decisions.

8. Cost/volume/profit (CVP) analysis _____   h. A menu item that is priced very low for the purpose of drawing large numbers of customers to the operation.

9. Contribution margin income statement _____   i. Food Cost % plus Variable Cost % used in calculating minimum sales point.

10. Contribution margin for overall operation	_____	j.	The total revenue generated by a facility divided by the number of seats in the dining area.
11. Minimum sales point (MSP)	_____	k.	A menu pricing and analysis system that compares goals of the foodservice operation to performance of individual menu items.
12. Minimum operating cost	_____	l.	The dollar sales volume required to justify staying open.
13. Budget	_____	m.	The amount that remains after the product cost of the menu item is subtracted from the item's selling price.
14. Long-range budget	_____	n.	The point at which operational expenses are exactly equal to sales revenue.
15. Annual budget	_____	o.	A forecast or estimate of projected revenue, expense, and profit for a defined accounting period. Often referred to as plan.
16. Achievement budget	_____	p.	Method that helps predict the sales dollars and volume required to achieve desired profit (or break-even) based on known costs.
17. Sales per seat	_____	q.	The contribution margin method of menu analysis.
18. Sales per square foot	_____	r.	A restaurant that offers a limited menu and is designed for the convenience of customers who want their food fast.
19. Yardstick method	_____	s.	The total revenue generated by a facility divided by the number of square feet the business occupies.

Discussion Questions

1. List and explain the three areas of analysis that will assist a manager in planning for profit.

_____

_____

_____

_____

2. Identify and explain the three main types of foodservice budgets.

_____

_____

_____

_____

3. List and explain three areas of a budget that should be monitored.

_____

_____

_____

_____

4. List the six different operational variables that can be analyzed using menu analysis.

_____

_____

_____

_____

5. List six strategies for reducing energy usage.

_____

_____

_____

_____

Quiz Yourself

Choose the letter of the best answer to the questions listed below.

1. A café has a check average of $18 and has variable costs per cover of $6.00. If its fixed costs are $58,000 for the month, the number of covers that must be sold to reach the monthly break-even point is:
   a. 6,000 covers
   b. 4,834 covers
   c. 3,254 covers
   d. 5,000 covers

2. Calculate the goal value for the following menu item: food cost % 47%; number sold 325; selling price $16.75; variable cost % 40%.
   a. 375.07
   b. 426.21
   c. 561.24
   d. 268.24

3. Given the following information, calculate the desired before-tax profit: tax rate 37%; desired after-tax profit $45,000; contribution margin % 75%.
   a. $26,486.27
   b. $69,874.36
   c. $71,428.57
   d. $18,697.65

4. Using the following information, calculate budgeted profit: budgeted revenue $36,458; actual revenue $40,365; budgeted expense $13,265.
   a. $43,957
   b. $23,193
   c. $33,652
   d. $56,496

5. Compute sales per seat using the following information: total sales $96,525; number of guests 5,103; available seats 354.
   a. $2,656.78
   b. $ 965.31
   c. $ 598.92
   d. $ 272.67

6. What is the formula for minimum sales point?
   a. Minimum labor cost x minimum operating cost
   b. Minimum labor cost/minimum operating cost
   c. Minimum operating cost x minimum labor cost
   d. Minimum labor cost/1 – minimum operating cost

7. Which of the following formulas is used to compute sales dollars to achieve desired after-tax profit?
   a. After-tax profit + fixed cost/contribution margin %
   b. Fixed costs + before-tax profit/contribution margin %
   c. Variable costs – fixed costs/before-tax profit
   d. After-tax profit/1 - tax rate

8. What is the formula for computing the contribution margin per menu item?
   a. Selling price + product cost
   b. Number of items x unit price
   c. Selling price – product cost
   d. Selling price/product cost

9. Which of the following formulas is used for computing average contribution margin per item?
   a. Total contribution margin/number of items sold
   b. Number of items sold x contribution margin
   c. Number of items sold + contribution margin
   d. Total sales/number of items sold

10. How do you calculate the break-even point in guests served?
    a. Total sales/break-even point
    b. Contribution margin x fixed cost %
    c. Fixed costs/total product costs
    d. Fixed costs/contribution margin per unit (guest)

11. A restaurant has a check average of $15, variable costs per cover of $9.00, and a tax rate of 40%. If its fixed costs are $80,000, and the restaurant owner desires an after-tax profit of $15,000, calculate the number of covers that must be sold to reach the desired profit.
    a. 17,500 covers
    b. 15,834 covers
    c. 13,334 covers
    d. 8,889 covers

12. Calculate the goal value for the following menu item: food cost % 35%; number sold 175; selling price $13.75; variable cost % 38%.
    a. 320.03
    b. 422.30
    c. 227.39
    d. 187.25

Chapter Answers to Key Terms & Concepts Review, Discussion Questions, and Quiz Yourself

Key Terms & Concepts Review

1. e	6. r	11. l	16. g
2. m	7. n	12. i	17. j
3. q	8. p	13. o	18. s
4. k	9. b	14. c	19. d
5. h	10. f	15. a	

Discussion Questions

1. List and explain the three areas of analysis that will assist a manager in planning for profit.
   - Menu analysis – Menu analysis is more than just numbers, it involves marketing, sociology, psychology, and emotions. Guests respond to menu copy, the description of the menu items, the placement of items on the menu, their menu price, and their current popularity.
   - Cost/volume/profit (CVP) analysis – Helps predict the sales dollars and volume required to achieve desired profit (or breakeven) based on the operations known costs.
   - Budget –Details the operational direction of your unit and your expected financial results (also known as the plan).

2. Identify and explain the three main types of foodservice budgets.
   - Long-range budget – Typically prepared for a period of three to five years. It provides a long-term view about where the operation should be going.
   - Annual budget – Typically prepared for a one-year period or, in some cases, one season.
   - Achievement budget – An achievement budget is always shorter range than an annual budget, perhaps a month or a week. It provides current operating information, and thus, assists in making current operational decisions.

3. List and explain three areas of a budget that should be monitored.
   - Revenue- If revenue falls below its projected levels, the impact on profit can be substantial. If revenue consistently exceeds your projections, the overall budget must be modified or the expenses associated with these increased sales will soon exceed budgeted amounts.

- Expense – Costs that are too high or too low may be a cause of concern. To help make an expense assessment quickly, some operators elect to utilize the yardstick method of calculating expense standards so determinations can be made as to whether variations in expenses are due to changes in sales volume or other reasons such as waste or theft.
- Profit – Budgeted profits must be realized if the operation is to provide adequate returns for owner and investor risk. A primary goal of management is to generate the profits necessary for the successful continuation of the business. Budgeting for these profits is a fundamental step in the process.

4. List the six different operational variables that can be analyzed using menu analysis.
   - Food cost percentage
   - Popularity
   - Contribution margin
   - Selling price
   - Variable expenses
   - Fixed expenses

5. List the six strategies for reducing energy usage.
   - Investigating the instillation of smart lighting systems that automatically turn off lights when storage areas are vacant.
   - Replacement of all incandescent lighting with an appropriate type of electric discharge lamp (such as fluorescent, mercury vapor, metal halide or sodium) wherever possible.
   - The use of dual-flush, low-flow or waterless toilets to reduce water waste.
   - Installing low-flow faucet aerators on all sinks to cut water usage by as much as 40%; from a standard 4 gallons per minute to a cost-saving 2.5 gallons a minute.
   - Implementation of an effective preventive maintenance program for all cooking equipment including frequent and accurate temperature recalibrations.
   - Reducing waste disposal costs by implementing effective source reduction plans as well as pre and post-production recycling efforts.

Quiz Yourself

1. b	7. b
2. a	8. c
3. c	9. a
4. b	10. d
5. d	11. a
6. d	12. b

Chapter 11

Maintaining and Improving the Revenue Control System

Learning Outcomes

At the conclusion of this chapter, you will be able to:

- Identify internal and external threats to revenue.

- Create effective countermeasures to combat internal and external theft.

- Establish and monitor a complete and effective revenue security system.

Study Notes

1. Revenue Security

- Errors in revenue collection can come from simple employee mistakes or, in some cases, outright theft by either guests or employees.

- In its simplest form, revenue control and security is a matter of matching products sold with funds received. Thus, an effective revenue security system ensures that the following five formulas reflect what really happens in your foodservice operation:

  1. Documented Product Requests = Product Issues

  2. Product Issues (by the kitchen) = Guest Charges

  3. Total Charges = Sales Receipts

  4. Sales Receipts = Sales (bank) Deposits

  5. Sales Deposits = Funds Available to Pay *Legitimate* Expenses (called Accounts Payable)

- The potential for guest or employee theft or fraud exists in all of these areas.

2. External Threats to Revenue Security

- A guest is said to have **walked**, or **skipped** a check when he or she has consumed a product but has left the foodservice operation without paying the bill. (See Figure 11.2 Steps to Reduce Guest "Walks" or "Skips")

- A second form of guest theft that you must guard against is that of fraudulent payment. This includes passing counterfeit money, bad checks, or most commonly, the use of invalid credit or debit cards.

- A **credit card** is simply a system by which banks loan money to consumers as the consumer makes purchases.

- **Travel and entertainment (T&E) cards** are a payment system by which the card issuer collects full payment from the card users on a monthly basis.

- A **debit card** is an extremely popular form of guest payment. In this system, the funds needed to cover the user's purchase are automatically transferred from the user's bank account to the entity issuing the debit card.

- If restaurant managers are to ensure that they collect all of the money they are due from payment card companies, they must effectively manage the **interface** (electronic connection) between the various payment card issuers and their restaurant.

- **Merchant service provider (MSP)** plays an important role as the restaurant's coordinator/manager of payment card acceptance and funds collection.

- A restaurant accepting payment cards does not actually "receive" immediate cash from its card sales but, rather, it will be credited via **electronic funds transfer (EFT)** the money it is due after all fees have been paid.

- If you agree to accept checks, you will likely experience some loss.

- In addition to skipping a bill and fraudulent payment attempts, the last method of guest theft you must be aware of is that used by the **quick-change artist**. A quick-change artist is a guest who, having practiced the routine many times, attempts to confuse the cashier; in his or her confusion, the cashier gives the guest too much change.

3. Internal Threats to Revenue Security

- Service personnel can use a variety of techniques to cheat an operation of a small amount at a time.

- One of the most common server theft techniques involves the omission of recording the guest's order.

- Complete revenue control is a matter of developing the checks and balances necessary to ensure that the value of products sold and the amount of revenue received equal each other.

- Servers can misrepresent the amount they charged guests.

- Food operations should require a written **guest check** recording each sale. A guest check is simply a written record of what the guest purchased and how much the guest was charged for the item(s).

- Paper guest checks should be recorded by number and then safely stored or destroyed, as management policy dictates.

- Another method of service personnel fraud is one in which the server gives the proper guest check to the guest, collects payment, and destroys the guest check but keeps the money.

- For this reason, many operators implement a **precheck/postcheck system** for guest checks.

- A **user workstation,** that is, a terminal records the items ordered and then displays the order in the production area. In some systems, the order may even be printed in the production area.

- Not all service personnel are dishonest, of course, but POS systems are especially designed to prevent dishonest employees from committing theft and fraud.

- It is important to remember, however, that even sophisticated POS systems hold the potential for employee fraud.

- If a cashier is responsible for the collection of money, several areas of potential fraud can exist. The cashier may collect payment from a guest but destroy the guest check that recorded the sale. Another method of cashier theft involves failing to finalize a sale recorded on the precheck, while pocketing the money.

- **Open checks** are those that have been used to authorize product issues from the kitchen or bar, but that have not been added to the operation's sales total.

- In addition to theft of your own business financial assets, the hospitality industry affords some employees the opportunity to defraud guests as well. Some techniques include:

  1. Charging guests for items not purchased, then keeping the overcharge.
  2. Changing the totals on credit card charges after the guest has left, or entering additional credit card charges and pocketing the cash difference.
  3. Misadding legitimate charges to create a higher than appropriate total, with the intent of keeping the overcharge.
  4. Purposely shortchanging guests when giving back change with the intent of keeping the extra change.
  5. Charging higher than authorized prices for products or services, recording the proper price, and then keeping the overcharge.

- Cashiers rarely steal large sums directly from the cash drawer because such theft is easily detected.

- Management can compare the sales recorded by the cash register with the money actually contained in the cash register. If it contains less than sales recorded, it is said to be **short,** if it contains more than sales recorded, it is said to be **over**.

- Consistent cash shortages may be an indication of employee theft or carelessness.

- If the POS system has a void key, a dishonest cashier could enter a sales amount, collect for it, and then void, or erase, the sale after the guest has departed.

- Another method of cashier theft involves the manipulation of complimentary meals or meal coupons.

- It is important to remember that even good revenue control systems present the opportunity for theft if management is not vigilant or if two or more employees conspire to defraud the operation.

- **Bonding** is simply a matter of management purchasing an insurance policy against the possibility that an employee will steal.

- If an employee has been bonded and an operation can determine that he or she was indeed involved in the theft of a specific amount of money, the operation will be reimbursed for the loss by the bonding company.

4. Developing the Revenue Security System

- An effective revenue security system will help you accomplish the following important tasks: verification of product issues, verification of guest charges, verification of sales receipts, verification of sales deposits and verification of account payable.

- In an ideal world, a product would be sold, its sale recorded, its selling price collected, the funds deposited in the foodservice operation's bank account, and the cost of providing the product would be paid for, all in a single step. Rapid advances in the area of computers and "smart" cards are making this a reality for more foodservice operators each day.

- The five-step process of revenue security is as follows:

> **Product Issues = Guest Charges**
> **= Sales Receipts = Sales Deposits**
> **= Funds Available for Accounts Payable**

- The key to verification of product issues in the revenue security system is to follow one basic rule: *No product should be issued from the kitchen or bar unless a permanent record of the issue is made.*

> **Documented Product Requests = Product Issues**

- When the production staff is required to distribute products only in response to a documented request, it is critical that those documented requests result in charges to the guest. *Product issues must equal guest charges.*

- Each guest check must be accounted for, and employees must know that they will be held responsible for each check they are issued.

> **Product Issues = Guest Charges**

- Sales receipts refer to actual revenue received by the cashier or other designated personnel, in payment for products served. *Both the cashier and a member of management must verify sales receipts.*

> **Total Charges = Sales Receipts**

- Sales receipts refer to all forms of revenue, such as cash, checks (if accepted), and bank (credit or debit) cards.

- In general, there are five basic payment arrangements in use in typical foodservice operations. They are as follows:
    1. Guest pays cashier.
    2. Guest pays at the table.
    3. Guest pays service personnel, who pay cashier.
    4. Guest pays service personnel, who have already paid cashier.
    5. Guest is direct billed.

- **Accounts receivable** is the term used to refer to guest charges that have been billed to the guest but not yet collected.

- In some cases, variations on the five payment systems presented can be put in place, such as the drink ticket, or coupon sold or issued in hotel reception areas for use at cocktail receptions.

- The deposit slip may be completed by a cashier or other clerical assistant, but management alone should bear the responsibility for monitoring the actual deposit of sales. This concept can be summarized as follows: *Management must personally verify all bank deposits*. This involves the actual verification of the contents of the deposit and the process of matching bank deposits with actual sales.

- **Embezzlement** is the term used to describe employee theft where the embezzler takes company funds he or she was entrusted to keep and diverts them to personal use.

- Falsification of bank deposits is a common method of embezzlement. To prevent this activity, you should take the following steps to protect your deposits:
    1. Make bank deposits of cash and checks daily if possible.
    2. Ensure that the person preparing the deposit is not the one making the deposit, unless you or the manager does both tasks. Also, ensure that the individual making the daily deposit is bonded.
    3. Establish written policies for completing **bank reconciliations**, the regularly scheduled comparison of the business's deposit records with the bank's acceptance records. Payment card funds transfers to a business's bank account should be reconciled each time they occur. Increasingly, cash and payment card reconciliations can be accomplished on a daily basis via the use of online banking features.
    4. Review and approve written bank statement reconciliations at least once each month.
    5. Change combinations on safes periodically and share the combinations with the fewest employees possible.
    6. Require that all cash handling employees take regular and uninterrupted vacations on a regular basis so that another employee can assume and uncover any improper practices.
    7. Employ an outside auditor to examine the accuracy of deposits on an annual basis.

- If verification of sales deposits is done correctly and no embezzlement is occurring, the following formula should hold true:

> **Sales Receipts = Sales Deposits**

- **Accounts payable,** as defined in this step, refers to the legitimate amount owed to a vendor for the purchase of products or services. The basic principle to be followed when verifying accounts payable is: *The individual authorizing the purchase should verify the legitimacy of the vendor's invoice before it is paid.*

- In a revenue system that is working properly, the following formula should be in effect:

> **Sales Deposits = Funds Available for Accounts Payable**

- You can protect your revenue from vendors who would attempt to defraud you. Here are steps you can take:

  1. Know your rights.
  2. Assign designated buyers and utilize purchase orders at all times.
  3. Check the documentation before paying bills.
  4. Train your staff.

- The five key principles of a revenue security system are as follows:

  1. No product shall be issued from the kitchen or bar unless a permanent record of the issue is made.
  2. Product issues must equal guest charges.
  3. Both the cashier and a supervisor must verify sales receipts.
  4. Management must personally verify all bank deposits.
  5. The individual authorizing the purchase should verify the legitimacy of the vendor's invoice before it is paid.

- It is possible to develop and maintain a completely manual revenue control system.

- When properly selected and understood, technology-enhanced systems can be a powerful ally in the cost control/revenue security system.

- When considering a POS system, that means choosing energy efficient systems designed for upgradability, expandability and long life. By using energy efficient POS equipment for longer periods of time, operating costs are reduced and landfill waste lessened.

- Some recently introduced POS solutions consume less energy than a standard 100-watt light bulb! Efficiency advancements such as these help operators save money from high energy costs, while also helping to relieve the stress of excess energy consumption on the environment.

5. Technology Tools

- Protecting sales revenue from external and internal threats of theft requires diligence and attention to detail.

- Software and specialized hardware now on the market that can help in this area includes those that:

  1. Maintain daily cash balances from all sources, including those of multiunit and international operations.
  2. Reconcile inventory reductions with product issues from kitchen.
  3. Reconcile product issues from kitchen with guest check totals.
  4. Reconcile guest check totals with revenue totals.
  5. Create over and short computations by server, shift, and day.
  6. Balance daily bank deposits with daily sales revenue and identify variances.
  7. Maintain database of returned checks.
  8. Maintain accounts receivable records.
  9. Maintain accounts payable records.
  10. Maintain records related to the sale and redemption of gift cards.
  11. Interface back office accounting systems with data compiled by the operation's POS system.
  12. Interface budgeting software with revenue generation software.
  13. Create income statements, statements of cash flows, and balance sheets.

- It is important to note that interfacing (connecting) the various software programs you select is very helpful.

Key Terms & Concepts Review

Match the key terms with their correct definitions.

1. Walk, or skip (the bill) _____   a. Cards in a payment system by which banks loan money to consumers as the consumers make purchases. The loans typically carry interest.

2. Quick-change artist _____   b. Checks that have been used to authorize product issues from the kitchen or bar, but that have not been added to the operation's sales total.

3. Non-sufficient funds (NSF) _____   c. Employees conspire to defraud the operation.

4. Counterfeit money _____   d. The legitimate amount owed to a vendor for products or services rendered.

5. Credit cards _____   e. A term used to describe a customer who has consumed a product, but leaves the foodservice operation without paying the bill.

6. Travel and Entertainment (T&E) cards _____   f. Purchasing an insurance policy to protect the operation in case of employee theft.

7. Debit cards _____   g. Provides for the electronic payment and collection of money and information.

8. Interface _____   h. Term used when the total amount of money in a cash drawer is more than the total amount of money that should be there based on sales receipts.

9. Merchant service provider (MSP) _____   i. The term used to describe theft of a type where the money, although legally possessed by the employee, is diverted to the employee by his or her fraudulent action.

10. Electronic funds transfer (EFT)	_____	j.	A guest who, having practiced the routine many times, attempts to confuse the cashier so that the cashier will give the guest too much change.
11. Guest check	_____	k.	The restaurant's coordinator / manager of payment card acceptance and funds collection, and who provides the electronic connection between payment card issuers and their merchants.
12. Pre-check/post-check system	_____	l.	Term used when the total amount of money in a cash drawer is less than the total amount of money that should be there based on sales receipts.
13. User workstation	_____	m.	Not enough money in a bank account to allow a check to be cashed.
14. Open check	_____	n.	A written record of what was purchased by the guest and how much the guest was charged for the item(s).
15. Short	_____	o.	The term used to refer to guest charges that have been billed to the guest but not yet collected.
16. Over	_____	p.	Cards in a payment system by which the funds needed to cover the user's purchase are automatically transferred from the user's bank account to the entity issuing the card.
17. Bonding	_____	q.	A computer terminal used only to ring up food and beverage orders.
18. Collusion	_____	r.	Cards in a payment system by which the card issuer collects full payment from the card users on a monthly basis. These card companies do not typically assess their users interest charges.
19. Credit card skimming	_____	s.	An imitation of currency intended to be passed off fraudulently as real money.

20. Accounts receivable	_____	t.	The server records the order on a guest check when the order is given to him or her by the guest. The products ordered by the guest and issued by the kitchen or bar should match the items and money collected by the cashier.
21. Embezzlement	_____	u.	Electronic connection for the purpose of sharing data.
22. Bank reconciliation	_____	v.	The term used to describe theft of credit card information used in an otherwise legitimate transaction.
23. Accounts payable	_____	w.	The regularly scheduled comparison of the business's deposit records with the bank's acceptance records.

Discussion Questions

1. List and explain the five formulas that will help a manager maintain an effective revenue security system.

_____

_____

_____

_____

2. Identify and explain two broad threats to revenue security systems.

_____

_____

_____

_____

3. List five of the eight steps that help to reduce guest walks, or skips.

_____

_____

_____

_____

4. List five tasks a manager must consider when developing a total revenue security system.

_____

_____

_____

_____

5. List two advantages of using energy efficient POS equipment.

_____

_____

_____

_____

Quiz Yourself

Choose the letter of the best answer to the questions listed below.

Use the information below to answer Questions 1 and 2.
Determine Tim's daily and weekly overage and shortage amounts.

Day	Sales Receipts	Guest Charges	Over/(Short)
Monday	$10,568.54	$10,540.20	
Tuesday	$11,698.82	$11,708.24	
Wednesday	$13,216.35	$13,220.97	
Thursday	$9,698.67	$9,705.21	
Friday	$14,987.63	$14,982.52	
Saturday	$15,468.15	$15,470.25	
Sunday	$11,568.74	$11,568.76	
Total	$87,206.90	$87,196.15	

1. What are Tim's total over/short results for the week?
   a. $15.25
   b. ($10.75)
   c. $10.75
   d. ($15.25)

2. Is Tim running his operation efficiently, and how often should Tim balance his sales receipts with his guest charges?
   a. No; he should check his balance every other day.
   b. Yes; he needs to keep up the good work.
   c. Yes; he should check his balances every week to keep on track.
   d. No; he needs to check his balances at the end of each shift.

3. Identify the formula that ensures that "The authorized purchaser must verify the legitimacy of accounts payable to be paid out of sales deposits."
   a. Documented Product Requests = Product Issues
   b. Product Issues = Guest Charges
   c. Total Charges = Sales Receipts
   d. Sales Receipts = Sales Deposits
   e. Sales Deposits = Funds Available for Accounts Payable

4. Identify the formula that ensures that "Both the cashier and a member of management must verify sales receipts."
   a. Documented Product Requests = Product Issues
   b. Product Issues = Guest Charges
   c. Total Charges = Sales Receipts
   d. Sales Receipts = Sales Deposits
   e. Sales Deposits = Funds Available for Accounts Payable

5. Identify the formula that ensures that "No product should be issued from the kitchen or bar unless a permanent record of the issue is made."
   a. Documented Product Requests = Product Issues
   b. Product Issues = Guest Charges
   c. Total Charges = Sales Receipts
   d. Sales Receipts = Sales Deposits
   e. Sales Deposits = Funds Available for Accounts Payable

6. Identify the formula that ensures that "Product issues must equal guest charges."
   a. Documented Product Requests = Product Issues
   b. Product Issues = Guest Charges
   c. Total Charges = Sales Receipts
   d. Sales Receipts = Sales Deposits
   e. Sales Deposits = Funds Available for Accounts Payable

7. Identify the formula that ensures that "Management must personally verify all bank deposits."
   a. Documented Product Requests = Product Issues
   b. Product Issues = Guest Charges
   c. Total Charges = Sales Receipts
   d. Sales Receipts = Sales Deposits
   e. Sales Deposits = Funds Available for Accounts Payable

8. What is the formula for ensuring the *total* revenue security system (in the proper order)?
   a. Funds available for accounts payable = sales deposits = sales receipts = guest charges = product issues
   b. Sales deposits = product issues = sales receipts = guest charges = funds available for accounts payable
   c. Sales receipts = sales deposits = guest charges = funds available for accounts payable = product issues
   d. Product issues = guest charges = sales receipts = sales deposits = funds available for accounts payable

9. What formula is used for determining overage and shortage amounts?
   a. Sales receipts – guest charges
   b. Guest charges/sales receipts
   c. Guest charges – sales receipts
   d. Sales receipts/guest charges

10. Which of the following is **not** a common method to minimize theft by service employees?
    a. Assign unique numbers to each guest check created
    b. Use a pre-check/post-check system
    c. Encourage employees to use shared POS passwords
    d. Close out open checks

11. Cards in a payment system by which the card issuer collects full payment from the card users on a monthly basis typically with no interest charges is called:
    a. Credit card
    b. Travel and entertainment card
    c. Debit card
    d. Disbursement card

12. Some employees may defraud guests by:
    a. Charging guests for items not purchased, then keeping the extra money
    b. Destroying the guest check or voiding the sale but keeping the money
    c. Entering another server's password in the POS and keeping the money
    d. Failing to finalize the sale and keeping the money

Chapter Answers to Key Terms & Concepts Review, Discussion Questions, and Quiz Yourself

Key Terms & Concepts Review

1. e	6. r	11. n	16. h	21. i
2. j	7. p	12. t	17. f	22. w
3. m	8. u	13. q	18. c	23. d
4. s	9. k	14. b	19. v	
5. a	10. g	15. l	20. o	

Discussion Questions

1. List and explain the five formulas that will help a manager maintain an effective revenue security system.
    *   Documented product requests = product issues. No product should be issued from the kitchen or bar unless a permanent record of the issue is made.
    *   Product issues = guest charges. Product issues must equal guest charges.
    *   Guest charges = sales receipts. Both the cashier and a member of management must verify sales receipts.
    *   Sales receipts = sales deposits. Management must personally verify all bank deposits.
    *   Sales deposits = accounts payable for legitimate expenses. The authorized purchaser must verify the legitimacy of accounts payable to be paid out of sales deposits.

2. Identify and explain two broad threats to revenue security systems.
    *   External threats to revenue security – Guests may pose external threats to revenue security by walking the check, being a quick-change artist, using stolen credit cards, having non-sufficient funds in their bank accounts, and using counterfeit money.
    *   Internal threats to revenue security – Cash is the most readily usable asset in a foodservice operation and can easily be stolen by employees. Service personnel may use a variety of techniques to cheat an operation of a small amount of money at a time.

3. List five of the eight steps that help to reduce guest walks, or skips.
   - If the custom of your restaurant is that guests order and consume their goods prior to your receiving payment, instruct servers to present the bill for the food promptly when the guests have finished.
   - If your facility has a cashier in a central location in the dining area, have that cashier available and visible at all times.
   - If your facility operates in such a manner that each server collects for his or her own guest's charges, instruct the servers to return to the table promptly after presenting the guest's bill to secure a form of payment.
   - Train employees to be observant of exit doors near rest rooms or other areas of the facility that may provide an unscrupulous guest the opportunity to exit the dining area without being easily seen.
   - If an employee sees a guest leave without paying the bill, management should be notified immediately.
   - Upon approaching a guest who has left without paying the bill, the manager should ask if the guest has inadvertently "forgotten" to pay. In most cases, the guest will then pay the bill.
   - Should a guest still refuse to pay or flee the scene, the manager should note the following on an incident report:
     - Number of guests involved
     - Amount of the bill
     - Physical description of the guest(s)
     - Vehicle description if the guests flee in a car, as well as the license plate number if possible
     - Time and date of the incident
     - Name of the server(s) who actually served the guest
   - If the guest is successful in fleeing the scene, the police should be notified. In no case should your staff member or managers be instructed to attempt to physically detain the guest. The liability that could be involved should an employee be hurt in such an attempt is far greater than the value of a skipped food and beverage bill.

4. List five tasks a manager must consider when developing a total revenue security system.
   - Verification of product issues
   - Verification of guest charges
   - Verification of sales receipts
   - Verification of sales deposits
   - Verification of accounts payable

5. List two advantages of using energy efficient POS equipment.
   - Operating costs are reduced and landfill waste lessened.
   - Operators save money from energy costs, while also helping to relieve the stress of excess energy consumption on the environment.

Quiz Yourself

1. c	7. d
2. d	8. d
3. e	9. a
4. c	10. c
5. a	11. b
6. b	12. a

Chapter 12

Global Dimensions of Cost Control

Learning Outcomes

At the conclusion of this chapter, you will be able to:

- Recognize the increasingly important role international expansion plays on the growth of foodservice companies.

- Identify important challenges faced by all foodservice professionals who are responsible for managing their company's international business operations.

- Determine how operational, cultural, financial, and technological challenges can affect the cost control-related activities of international foodservice managers.

Study Notes

1. Multinational Foodservice Operations

- The global expansion of the restaurant industry really should come as no surprise to anybody working in this industry. This is so because travel, tourism, and the sampling of international cuisines have historically been integral parts of the hospitality industry.

- While Coca-Cola and McDonald's are among the best known, many other food service companies now operate in the international market and the number doing so increases each year.

- Burger King, Wendy's, Hilton, Dave and Busters, Hooters, T.G.I. Friday's, Mrs. Fields, Dunkin Donuts, Baskin Robbins, Pizza Hut, Marriott, Taco Bell, Aramark, TCBY, and Rainforest Cafe are just a few examples of the increasingly large number of U.S.-based restaurant companies expanding internationally.

2. Managing in a Global Economy

- Most companies want to exercise a specific level of control over their international operations. The control may be quite significant or it may be advisory in nature only.

- As a professional in the hospitality industry, there are a variety of reasons why you might be assigned the responsibility of controlling and monitoring costs in one or more of your company's international operations.

  - Your education and past work history give you the experience you need to succeed in the job.
  - No local staff (in the foreign country) is currently qualified to assume the responsibility.
  - Your responsibilities include the training of local staff.
  - Local persons are being trained for positions that will ultimately replace the need for your assistance, but they are not yet qualified to assume 100% responsibility.
  - Your employer wants to instill a global perspective in you (and other) managers.
  - It is in the company's best long-term interest to improve the cultural understanding between managers and employees in the company's various international components.
  - An international assignment is considered an integral part of your professional development process.
  - There is an interest in obtaining tighter administrative control over a foreign division or addressing and correcting a significant problem.
  - There are property start-up, operating, or other issues that require long-term on-site management direction to properly address the issues.

- Experienced **expatriate** (a citizen of one country who is working in another country) managers and those whose offices are located in their home country but who travel extensively to their foreign assignments report that they sometimes confront issues in one or more of the following areas:

  - **Language**
    While English is widely spoken in many parts of the world, in many cases it will not be the primary language of the restaurant's employees, and thus expatriate managers must be sensitive to the variety of issues language barriers and the direct translation of languages may present.

  - **Local Governmental Entities**
    Routine items such as operating permits and permissions to do business may be slower in coming than in the United States. As well, local customs may dictate that money, paid directly or indirectly to governmental officials, may accompany the granting of these permissions.

  - **Facilities**
    Foodservice operators will find it more difficult to build, service, and maintain their physical facilities in foreign countries. This is especially true if the company has not identified a dependable, cost-effective, and local service representative for the building they occupy or the major equipment they utilize.

197

- **Employees**
  The local labor force that is available to international managers can vary greatly from one area of the world to another. In addition, employee attitudes toward gender equality, appropriate dress, work ethic, religious tolerance, and the rights of minorities are all areas that may present significant challenges to you as an international food service manager.

- **Suppliers**
  The actual operation of an international food service unit can be challenging for a variety of reasons. Among these challenges is the potential unreliability of the units food **supply chain**. If a restaurant is dependent upon a unique product that is prepared in another location, frozen, and then shipped to the unit, a dependable refrigerated storage and delivery company will likely be of critical importance if a high level of food quality is to be maintained.

3. Cost Control Challenges in Global Operations

- One convenient way to view international cost control–related challenges is by categorizing them as one of the following types:

  - Operational challenges
  - Cultural challenges
  - Financial challenges
  - Technological challenges

- **Operational Challenges**

  - The cost control issues encountered by expatriate hospitality managers can be related to what is done, when things are done, and exactly how they are done.

  - U.S. companies are accustomed to the **day parts** that have traditionally been defined as the breakfast, lunch, and dinner periods, in other countries the names for, and the times of, these day parts may vary significantly.

  - For those managers who have learned food production techniques using the **British Imperial** (U.S. Standard) **measurement system** of ounces, pounds, gallons, and tablespoons, converting recipes and purchasing standards to the metric system can often seem challenging.

- Other important areas that can be greatly affected include:
  - Marketing
  - Menu Planning
  - Pricing
  - Safety standards
  - Purchasing
  - Receiving
  - Beverage production and service
  - Equipment selection and maintenance
  - Utility (natural resource) management

- According to Pacific Gas and Electric's Food Service Technology Center, 80 percent of the $10 billion annual energy bill for the commercial food service sector is expended by inefficient food cooking, holding, and storage equipment.

- Energystar, the US government operated web site devoted to energy efficiency, reports that the average food service operator who invests strategically can cut his or her utility costs 10 to 30 percent without sacrificing service, quality, style, or comfort.

- On its website, Energystar also points out that "the money you save on operating costs adds to what you get to keep, so saving 20% on energy operating costs can increase your profit as much as one-third".

- **Cultural Challenges**

  - **Culture** can be defined as the customary beliefs, social norms, and characteristic traits of a racial, religious, or social group.

  - As a manager, it will be your responsibility to ensure the smooth operation of your facilities by fairly addressing issues that may arise.

  - Expatriate managers who succeed best do so by demonstrating the real respect and understanding for local culture that is most often missing in less successful international managers.

  - Utilizing the following guidelines can help you effectively meet cultural challenges.
    - Foster an environment that encourages open discussion.
    - Encourage interaction.
    - Celebrate diversity.
    - Foster a healthy understanding of group identity.
    - Model appropriate behavior.

- **Financial Challenges**

  - It is a fundamental principle of accounting that the financial results of a business should be reported in an identifiable monetary unit.

  - A **monetary unit** is simply defined as a specific and recognized currency denomination. The reporting of cash sales may be complex in international companies because of a potential variety of monetary units being used.

  - Credit, debit, and bank card sales (which constitute a large portion of many restaurants' total sales) create further complications because the company's merchant service provider must apply an **exchange rate** (to convert the value of one currency to another) before the funds can be credited.

- **Technological Challenges**

  - Carefully consider the following essential elements before selecting and purchasing any technological enhancement to your existing cost control efforts.

  - **Cost**
    When it is possible to demonstrate that the technology-related purchase will pay for itself (such as in reduced labor or product cost) relatively quickly, the decision to buy can be an easy one. If the cost of the tool exceeds its value to your operations, it likely should not be purchased.

  - **Complexity**
    Some technology systems are so advanced that their implementation and routine operation requires very high levels of skills. Difficulties can be reduced or eliminated through the implementation of thorough training programs.

  - **System Warranty/Maintenance**
    Because technology items are machines, they need routine maintenance and can break down. Items of particular importance to you will be:
    - A listing of precisely which items are covered under the terms of the warranty
    - The length of the warranty
    - The allowable charges for repair service for non-warranty-covered items
    - Expected response time of the service/repair technicians

  - **Upgradability**
    While it is difficult to predict what new technological developments may occur in the future, it is true that advancements that are compatible with your current system will likely prove to be less expensive than those that require completely new software, hardware, or communication devices.

- **Reliability**
  There are two areas of importance which are: reliability of the product or service, and reliability of the vendor. A variety of factors can influence vendor reliability including location, experience, quality of service staff, response time, and reputation.

- It is simply not possible to know about every technological advance that could directly affect your international business. You can, however, stay abreast of the commercial application of these advances.

- Choices for continuing education in this area are varied but most foodservice managers can choose from one or more of the following methods:

  - **Trade Shows/Professional Associations**
    These associations typically serve the certification, educational, social, and legislative goals of their members. Trade shows are an extremely efficient way to see the product offerings of a large number of vendors in a very short time.

  - **Publications**
    Technology and its application have become such a large part of the editorial interest of these publications that a special technology editor is employed to monitor technological changes that could be of interest to the publication's readers.

  - **Current Vendors**
    Your current technology suppliers should be a valuable source of no-cost information. An added advantage of working with your current technology suppliers is the fact that the new systems they develop are likely to be compatible with those systems you already have and maintain.

  - **Competitive Vendors**
    Identifying your current vendor's strongest and best competitors is a good way to monitor advances in technology. Competitor visits can help you quickly identify improvements in procedures and features that your own vendor may have overlooked or dismissed.

  - **Your Own Organization**
    Often, large international companies will produce newsletters, conduct in-service training, or hold regularly scheduled conventions that can be a source of information on changing technology.

Key Terms & Concepts Review

Match the key terms with their correct definitions.

1. Expatriate _____

2. Supply chain _____

3. Day parts _____

4. British imperial (measurement system) _____

5. Culture _____

6. Monetary unit _____

7. Exchange rate _____

8. Professional trade association _____

a. A citizen of one country who is working in another country.

b. (U.S. Standard) Imperial measurement system of weights and measures including ounces, pounds, gallons, tablespoons, etc.

c. A specific currency denomination, e.g. US dollar, British pound, Japanese yen.

d. Associations that typically serve the certification, educational, social, and legislative goals of its members. Such associations hold annual gatherings, and, in conjunction with these meetings, they invite exhibitors who sell products and services of interest to interact with their members at trade shows.

e. To convert the value of one currency to another.

f. The distribution system that gets products from the primary source (i.e. grower) to the foodservice operation.

g. In the US, breakfast, lunch and dinner periods.

h. The customary beliefs, social norms, and characteristic traits of a racial, religious, or social group.

Discussion Questions

1. List and explain five problems that an expatriate manager may run into while working in a foreign country.

_____

_____

_____

_____

2. List four types of cost control challenges in global operations.

_____
_____
_____
_____

3. List five different essential elements that management should examine before selecting and purchasing any technological enhancement to existing cost control efforts.

_____
_____
_____
_____

4. Identify and explain five different methods that a foodservice manager can use to monitor developments in cost control technology.

_____
_____
_____
_____

5. List two advantages of commitment to green operations that Energystar has indicated on its website.

_____
_____
_____
_____

Quiz Yourself

Choose the letter of the best answer to the questions listed below.

1. Which of the following is an essential element that management should examine before selecting and purchasing any technological enhancement to existing cost control efforts?
   a. Cost
   b. Complexity
   c. Reliability
   d. All of the above

2. A currency is converted from one country to another at a(n):
   a. Exchange rate
   b. Dollar rate
   c. Money rate
   d. Coin rate

3. Which of the following issues might an expatriate manager confront while working in another country?
   a. Facilities issues
   b. Employee issues
   c. Supplier issues
   d. All of the above

4. In order to effectively meet cultural challenges, a manager should:
   a. Keep people from interacting too much to avoid arguments
   b. Minimize the obvious differences in people
   c. Foster an understanding of cultural group identity
   d. Discourage open discussion of differences

5. The British Imperial measurement system includes all of the following *except*:
   a. Ounces
   b. Gallons
   c. Tablespoons
   d. Grams

6. Any proposed improvement in technology should be considered in light of its ability to do all of the following *except*:
   a. Enhance guest satisfaction
   b. Significantly increase complexity
   c. Reduce costs through improved decision making
   d. Increase employee or management productivity

7. For international managers seeking to electronically interface their individual units with their corporate office, which of the following considerations would be *most* important?
   a. Vendor stock price
   b. Vendor attitude
   c. Vendor service reliability
   d. Vendor pricing

8. Professional trade associations typically serve the following needs of their members *except*:
   a. Educational
   b. Psychological
   c. Social
   d. Legislative

9. Employee issues that may present challenges to international managers include:
   a. Gender equality
   b. Work ethic
   c. Minority rights
   d. Religious tolerance
   e. All of the above

10. A specific currency denomination is known as a(n):
    a. Monetary unit
    b. Exchange rate
    c. Conversion factor
    d. Paper money

11. As a professional in the hospitality industry, you might be assigned the responsibility of controlling and monitoring costs in one or more of your company's international operations because:
    a. An international assignment is considered an integral part of your professional development process
    b. There is an interest in obtaining tighter administrative control over a foreign division or addressing and correcting a significant problem
    c. There are property start-up, operating, or other issues that require long-term onsite management direction to properly address the issues
    d. All of the above

12. Cost control challenges in global operations include:
    a. Operational challenges
    b. Cultural challenges
    c. Financial challenges
    d. All of the above

Chapter Answers to Key Terms & Concepts Review, Discussion Questions, and Quiz Yourself

Key Terms & Concepts Review

1. a   5. h
2. f   6. c
3. g   7. e
4. b   8. d

Discussion Questions

1. List and explain five problems that an expatriate manager may run into while working in a foreign country.
    *   Language – While English is widely spoken in many parts of the world, in many cases it will not be the primary language of a restaurant's employees, and thus expatriate managers must be sensitive to the variety of issues language barriers and the direct translation of languages may present.
    *   Local governmental entities – Routine items such as operating permits and permissions to do business may be slower in coming than in the United States.
    *   Facilities – Foodservice operators will find it more difficult to build, service, and maintain their physical facilities in foreign countries.
    *   Employees – The local labor force that is available to international managers can vary greatly from one area of the world to another.
    *   Suppliers – The actual operation of an international food service unit can be challenging for a variety of reasons. Among these challenges is the potential unreliability of the unit(s) food supply chain.

2. List four types of cost control challenges in global operations.
    *   Operational challenges
    *   Cultural challenges
    *   Financial challenges
    *   Technological challenges

3. List five different essential elements that management should examine before selecting and purchasing any technological enhancement to existing cost control efforts.
    *   Cost
    *   Complexity
    *   System warranty/maintenance
    *   Upgradeability
    *   Reliability

4. Identify and explain five different methods that a foodservice manager can use to monitor developments in cost control technology.

- Trade shows/professional associations – These associations typically serve the certification, educational, social, and legislative goals of their members.
- Publications – Technology and its application have become such a large part of the editorial interest of these publications that a special technology editor is employed to monitor technological changes that could be of interest to the publication's readers.
- Current vendors – Your current technology suppliers should be a valuable source of no-cost information.
- Competitive vendors - Identifying your current vendor's strongest and best competitors is a good way to monitor advances in technology.
- Your own organization – Often, large international companies will produce newsletters, conduct in-service training, or hold regularly scheduled conventions that can be a source of information on changing technology.

5. List two advantages of commitment to green operations that Energystar has indicated on its website.

- Reducing utility costs 10 to 30 percent without sacrificing service, quality, style, or comfort.
- The money you save on operating costs adds to what you get to keep, so saving 20% on energy operating costs can increase your profit as much as one-third.

Quiz Yourself

1. d	7. c
2. a	8. b
3. d	9. e
4. c	10. a
5. d	11. d
6. b	12. d